Applying
the Sermon

How to Balance Biblical Integrity
and Cultural Relevance

DANIEL OVERDORF

Applying the Sermon: How to Balance Biblical Integrity and Cultural Relevance

© 2009 by Daniel Overdorf

Published by Kregel Publications, a division of Kregel, Inc., P.O. Box 2607, Grand Rapids, MI 49501.

ISBN 978-0-8254-3447-1

Printed in the United States of America

09 10 11 12 13 / 5 4 3 2 1

To my father, Ken Overdorf,
who has faithfully preached
the Word for more than fifty years.

Contents

Foreword

I read a lot of books on preaching. Since I'm a preacher and a professor of homiletics, I figure I should do everything I can to keep up with the field.

Much of my reading is "dutiful," as I stick with a book over a period of days or weeks until I finish it. But *Applying the Sermon* turned out to be a "page-turner"—with insightful content and a captivating style—and I finished it in one sitting.

We have few resources of this length and depth on the topic of application. Daniel Overdorf is certainly qualified to write on the subject. He has done graduate work at respected institutions, is committed to the best kind of biblical preaching, and has both the academic and pastoral experience to write substantively and practically.

He begins, appropriately, by insisting that before we apply, we must first discover what God was saying to the original readers through the original author. With this biblical foundation solidly in place, he then takes on such gutsy issues as:

- How much of application is my job, and how much is the Spirit's?
- When does a biblical example (description) become a normative pattern (prescription)?
- How can I avoid applications that spiritualize, moralize, trivialize, or promise the unpromised?

You will find stimulating thought and helpful examples all through this book. You will go through a process for developing applications that will enable you to vividly and concretely connect God's truth to contemporary life.

And as the power of God's Word takes fresh grip on you, you'll be excited and impatient for Sunday, eager to share with your people how their good God is speaking directly into their lives.

—DONALD R. SUNUKJIAN, PH.D., TH.D.
Professor of Homiletics and Chair of the
Christian Ministry and Leadership Department at
Talbot School of Theology

Acknowledgments

I want to thank Jim Weaver and Kregel Publications for giving this book the opportunity to find its way onto preachers' bookshelves; Haddon Robinson, Will Willimon, Tom Long, Vic Pentz, and Bob Russell for sharing your wisdom and allowing me to use it in the book; Drew Keane, proofreader extraordinaire, for the hours invested in helping me polish the manuscript; and my family—Carrie, Peyton, Tyler, and Claire—for your constant patience and love.

Introduction

Sermon application frightens me.

I find some comfort knowing that others share my fears. Will Willimon, author of more than fifty books dealing with preaching and pastoral ministry, and named in a Baylor University study as one of the twelve most effective preachers in the English-speaking world, was gracious enough to talk with me about sermon application. "You're working in one of the most dangerous areas of homiletics," he began, "where we preachers most often fall off the wagon."[1]

Haddon Robinson, author of the modern classic *Biblical Preaching,* and like Willimon named in the Baylor University study, quipped, "Sermon application is like peeling an onion. At first it seems easy, but as you go through layer after layer all you have is tears."[2]

Even the most seasoned homileticians balk at sermon application. Why? Because application requires preachers to toss a grenade-like "thus saith the Lord" into people's lives and to do so repeatedly.

No other aspect of the preaching process leaves me shaking with such intensity in my homiletical boots.

---

1. Interview conducted with Will Willimon at Duke University in Durham, North Carolina.
2. Haddon Robinson, "The Preacher and the Message" class notes, Gordon-Conwell Theological Seminary, May 27, 2002.

Exegesis brings its complications. But, for the most part, I can stand in the pulpit on a weekly basis, confident in the accuracy of my hermeneutical arrows. Exegesis involves a mixture of science and art—with the right tools, knowledge of the proper techniques, and sufficient elbow grease, a preacher can discover the meaning of a text with moderate assurance.

As for illustrations, I occasionally grope for just the right story or quote, but thanks to the abundance of materials available—in experience, in print, and on the Internet—I generally have more illustrative material than I can use. Illustrating sermons compares to picking through a buffet. It's all there; we simply must discern what will best whet listeners' appetites.

Introductions? Conclusions? Transitions? None are painless, but with enough practice and effort most preachers can achieve relative competence with these.

Then we arrive at the issue of application. Application is neither science nor art, and it barely resembles a buffet. Practice and effort spur some progress, but it is not always significant. I seldom enter the pulpit confident in my sermon's applications.

When we dare to tread in people's lives—not just in broad, vague platitudes, but by nuzzling up to listeners' inmost attitudes and decisions and actions—we dare to tread in the footsteps of the prophets and apostles. We dare to meddle, to pry, and to nudge (and not always so gently!). And we dare to do this in the name of God.

Why tread on such dangerous ground? Ultimately, we venture into application because we hope our preaching will make a difference in listeners' lives. We pry and nudge because, as much fear as it induces, most homileticians agree that effective preaching necessarily includes application.[3] God's Word

---

3. Some shy away from the term *application,* an issue we will discuss in chapter 2; however, most agree that in some manner sermons must effectively relate biblical teaching to contemporary life.

entered history in an effective way—challenging individuals and communities toward transformation. "The preacher's challenge," Sidney Greidanus explains, "is to let the word of God address people today just as explicitly and concretely as it did in biblical times."[4] Herein lie the problem and the basis of a journey I propose we take together.

Effective preaching includes application that, first, allows the Word of God to speak (which requires biblical integrity) and, second, allows the Word of God to speak as explicitly and concretely today as it did originally (which requires contemporary relevance). Preachers often "fall off the wagon," as Willimon put it, because our application lacks one or both of these elements.

If this holds true, then we need to discover a way—a tool, perhaps—that will help us develop application with biblical integrity and contemporary relevance.

I want to invite you to journey with me toward the development of such a tool. We will begin by defining terms such as *effective preaching, sermon application, biblical integrity,* and *contemporary relevance* (chap. 1). Then, we will discuss how to cooperate with the Holy Spirit to apply texts to our listeners' lives (chap. 2). Next, we will define what the Bible teaches and exemplifies in relation to our topic (chap. 3). Following this, we will examine the exegetical and homiletical land mines that often endanger application (chap. 4). Then, we will gather all we've learned and mold it into a tool to help us develop sermon application with biblical integrity and contemporary relevance (chaps. 5–7). Finally, we will discuss ways to integrate this application into actual sermons (chap. 8). An appendix will offer a sample sermon manuscript that demonstrates the principles we will have discussed.

---

4. Sidney Greidanus, *The Modern Preacher and the Ancient Text* (Grand Rapids: Eerdmans, 1988), 159.

Along the way we will talk with five of the world's most respected preachers about sermon application. Each chapter will include snippets drawn from face-to-face conversations I enjoyed with the following homileticians.

Will Willimon has taught and written extensively in the field of homiletics. His reputation as a straight-shooting intellectual intrigued me. I felt sure Dr. Willimon would stretch me and my assumptions about sermon application. He did.

Just weeks before Dr. Willimon resigned from his position with Duke University to serve as a bishop in the United Methodist Church, he met with me in a small conference room in the basement of the massive, cathedral-like chapel at Duke.

Tom Long followed in Fred Craddock's shoes as the Bandy Professor of Preaching at Emory University's Candler School of Theology in Atlanta. His books, articles, and lectures have informed numerous preachers on the finer points of homiletics. Combining intellect, form, charisma, and even a voice many envy, Long provides a homiletical model we would do well to emulate.

I met with Long in his unassuming office—strewn with books, magazines, and graded papers—which sits at the end of an upstairs hallway in the Candler chapel. He seemed as eager as I was to tackle the difficult subject of sermon application.

Haddon Robinson serves as the Harold J. Ockenga Distinguished Professor of Preaching at Gordon-Conwell Theological Seminary. If you asked, "Who wrote the book on expository preaching?" the most common answer in our generation would probably be Robinson. One hundred and twenty seminaries and Bible colleges around the world use *Biblical Preaching*, Robinson's premier work, as a homiletics textbook.

I spoke with Robinson over sandwiches at Gordon-Conwell in a quiet room down the hallway from the seminary's cafeteria.

Bob Russell recently retired from his role as Senior Minister of Southeast Christian Church in Louisville, Kentucky, which draws close to twenty thousand attendees each weekend. Currently he ministers to churches and church leaders through retreats, seminars, and a mentoring ministry. When I asked around to see who preachers and homiletics professors look to as the experts in sermon application, Russell's name frequently topped the list. In fact, *Preaching* magazine's 2004 book of the year, which categorized the communication styles of today's most respected preachers, labeled Bob Russell "The Practical Applicator."[5]

On the day of our appointment, I drove to Louisville and onto the impressive Southeast Christian Church campus. Russell met me with a warm handshake in a third-floor conference room.

Vic Pentz preaches at the Presbyterian Church U.S.A.'s largest congregation—Peachtree Presbyterian in Atlanta. Three thousand people gather each weekend to worship and to hear Dr. Pentz's skillful exposition of God's Word. Thousands more tune in weekly to the church's television and Internet broadcasts.

Pentz is a wordsmith with a knack of uncovering the Bible's relevance for contemporary culture. We sat on couches in his office, chitchatted for a moment about the Atlanta Braves, and then discussed sermon application.

I offer my sincere appreciation to these five gentlemen for so graciously sharing their time and wisdom.

---

5. Dave Stone, *Refining Your Style: Learning from Respected Communicators* (Loveland, CO: Group Publishing, 2004).

CHAPTER ONE

Preaching Effectively

We begin our journey with an assumption: Effective preaching includes application that preserves biblical integrity while pursuing contemporary relevance. We will debate the accuracy of this statement later; but before entering such a discussion, we should define the key terms contained in the assumption.

Effective Preaching

My most frightening moment as a preacher came not in the pulpit but in the fellowship hall. A young mother grabbed my arm and pulled me aside. "I need to tell you something about the sermon you preached last month," she began with a grin.

My mind traced back through the manila folders in my file cabinet, trying to recall what on earth I had preached the month before. I could recall nothing more than a couple fuzzy titles and remnants of stories.

"You talked about greed and contentment," she explained, probably sensing my hazy memory. "You said that 'a man's life does not consist in the abundance of his possessions.'"

"Ah yes," I thought. "Rich Fool. Bigger Barns. Rich toward God."

"My husband and I have been thinking about moving. We have a nice house, and we like it just fine; but he got a big raise, and we thought it would be fun to buy a bigger house. But after your sermon we felt convicted. And, in the following weeks, God worked through some other conversations and some things we read and—well—we decided we're already very blessed and we can be more than content right where we are. We're going to increase our giving instead of our mortgage payment. I just wanted to tell you that your sermon made a difference!"

I gulped.

You mean people actually listen and consider what I say? They make decisions and change plans based (at least in part) on what they heard in a sermon?

Not every sermon bears such evident fruit—I can count on one hand conversations I've had like the one above. Even so, this fruit continues to represent the goal of preaching effectively.

Effective preaching, stated simply, has an effect. It makes a difference. It changes hearts. It influences decisions. It equips servants. It spurs obedience.

Effective preaching unleashes the Word, not only to inform, but also to transform. Such preaching draws its power from the

> *Effective preaching spurs transformation.*

Word of God, which beyond simply conveying information "is useful for teaching, rebuking, correcting and training in righteousness" (2 Tim. 3:16). Elsewhere Paul instructed Timothy to teach sound doctrine that stood in contrast to the false teaching that had infiltrated the church in Ephesus (1 Tim. 1:3–10; 6:3–20). For what purpose should Timothy teach this doctrine? For the sake of knowledge? To prepare the Ephesian believers for an academic final exam concerning the intricacies of Christian dogma? No, "the goal of this command is love, which comes from a pure heart and a good conscience and a sincere faith" (1 Tim. 1:5). Christian doctrine leads to Christ-like behavior.

Vic Pentz teaches that in "creative tension between Word and world transformation occurs. While worldly influences shape people toward conformity, preaching summons them to their unique destiny as God's children."[1] God predestined that believers will be "conformed to the likeness of his Son" (Rom. 8:29). Effective preaching spurs listeners toward this destiny, even if it's just one step closer.

Sermon Application

If effective preaching makes an impact, then sermon application includes those elements of the sermon that explain or demonstrate what particular impact a sermon should have. "Application," writes Calvin Miller, "is the science of what's happening now. Without it the sermon is at best a diagnostic device in which the preacher points out what is wrong with the world and then says the benediction. Diagnosis is analytical. Application is prescriptive. Without application, there is no sermon. Application is what gets the Sermon off the Mount, and down into the valley where the toilers live out their days."[2] Application leads the listener to imagine how the truth of the text makes a difference where they live.

The preacher might offer this application in the form of explanation or in the form of demonstration.

Explanation

Sometimes application involves a straightforward explanation of how biblical teaching should impact lives. When explaining the application, the preacher speaks directly to the

---

1. Victor Pentz, "Preaching to Effect Transformation," (D.Min. diss., Fuller Theological Seminary, 1991), 1.

2. Calvin Miller, *Preaching: The Art of Narrative Exposition* (Grand Rapids: Baker, 2006), 79.

listener concerning the implications of the text. The application includes first-person ("we") and second-person ("you") admonitions. "Because of what this text teaches," the preacher explains, "you might . . ."

How can we make certain our preaching is transformational?

Will Willimon: Our sermons are only transformational when we put them in God's hands. I really believe that preaching is a miracle. It is an act of God. It begins, "And God said . . ." If God does not speak, then all of our flailings are for naught.

Once at Duke I preached from the proverb, "Better than silver or gold is a good reputation. A good name is better than riches." In the sermon I said, "None of you believe that—if you did you wouldn't be here at Duke."

A kid came down afterward and said, "I really appreciated that."

"What did you like about it?" I asked.

"It was just so comforting."

"Comforting isn't what I was going for, I don't think."

"I'm going to call my father tonight and tell him that after that sermon, I'm not going to law school. I'm going into elementary school teaching. And if he doesn't like it, he can go jump in a lake."

I said, "Don't mention me when you talk to your dad!"

I just stumbled back to my office, thinking, "That's unbelievable!" Proverbs to me represents total establishment, bourgeoisie, middle class, helpful hints for homemakers . . . no redemption. But, in God's hands, that stuff becomes dynamite.

There've been many Sundays when God has just wrenched a sermon out of my hands. I had a goal, a plan for reaching that goal, and God said, "Give me that weak sermon. Let me do something with it. I'll work it up."

A sermon by Duane Litfin, "Riding the Wind of God," provides an example. Basing his message on Psalm 127, Litfin taught that Christians should focus life on those matters that hold eternal significance. He then explained how this principle might apply.

> For example, if you are a business or professional person, think of how you are spending your life. If you are spending your time and energy to build a company or a position or a practice, in order to become affluent, to grow in influence and prestige and personal comfort, there is nothing that I know of to suggest that Jesus Christ is the least bit interested in your success. You're on your own. You are involved in a project of your own choosing, not his.
>
> On the other hand, if you are committed to the business or professional world in order to use the gifts God has given you to build Christ's kingdom, then you have enlisted in one of God's choicest projects. Your time and energy are being invested with eternal dividends. Your efforts will be directed toward functioning as a beachhead for righteousness, and for the gospel of Jesus Christ, wherever God has put you. Like Daniel shining in a pagan world, personal profit will have become unimportant; the glory of God, manifested in all you do and say and demonstrated in the sheer excellence and integrity of your work and witness, becomes your priority.[3]

Sermon application explains or demonstrates how biblical teaching should impact the lives of contemporary listeners.

---

3. Duane Litfin, "Riding the Wind of God," in *Biblical Sermons: How Twelve Preachers Apply the Principles of Biblical Preaching*, ed. Haddon Robinson (Grand Rapids: Baker, 1989), 102.

Litfin explained, in a straightforward manner, how Psalm 127 might impact his listeners.

Demonstration

While the preacher sometimes might explain the application, on other occasions the preacher might demonstrate, by means of a real-to-life illustration, how biblical teaching should impact listeners' lives. Preachers often use illustrations to shed light on truth, helping listeners understand a principle. Such illustrations do not fall into the category of application. In other cases, however, illustrations demonstrate how a teaching that is already understood should impact the life of a listener. In these instances, illustrations do fall into the category of application.

Application via demonstration usually comes in third person—instead of "we" and "you," the preacher speaks of "him," "her," or "they," or uses particular names.

> For example, I recently preached from Romans 12 concerning believers using their gifts and abilities to serve the kingdom. I decided the most effective means of applying the text would come through demonstration—two illustrations drawn from our church community. God made Chad Walker, one of our church members, into an athlete. Just look at Chad, shake his hand, and you'll have no doubt—Chad is an athlete. He was recently inducted into the West Georgia University Athletic Hall of Fame for his outstanding performance as a wide receiver on the football team. Do you know how Chad serves the kingdom with his abilities? He leads our church's involvement in a children's basketball league. He works with two other churches. Six hundred kids from the community are involved in this league. God equipped Chad, and Chad has a great time using his abilities for the kingdom.

God equipped Alan Turner with leadership abilities. Alan is a quiet fella, but he has a gift of taking a room full of people and accomplishing something. He also has a passion to win the world for Jesus Christ. So, Alan leads our Missions Ministry Team. They oversee a budget of $150,000 a year that supports works from India to Jamaica to Mexico to our backyard. This year they planned two mission trips that enabled church members to visit and assist mission works. God equipped Alan, and Alan finds great fulfillment using his gifts for the kingdom.

I could share countless similar stories from churches across the world. Could I share your story? If I preached on this same topic a year from now, could we look to you as an example?

The demonstrations may not necessarily involve true stories like those above; a preacher might imagine circumstances or scenarios and then paint these pictures in listeners' minds. For example, a preacher might say, "Imagine a young woman blessed with a mind for administration. She wants to serve God but does not have the abilities needed to serve in the most obvious ways. She can't sing in tune or play an instrument, she has nightmares about the possibility of teaching the preschool Sunday school class, and she is far too shy to serve as a greeter. One Tuesday afternoon, however, she stops by the church office just when the secretary is pulling her hair out in frustration, unable to make heads or tails of the recent church financial report." Though such imagined scenarios do not tell of true, actual happenings, they are real-to-life and effectively demonstrate for listeners how a biblical teaching can impact their lives.

Effective application often includes demonstration because, as Donald Sunukjian teaches, "Unless the listeners get a mental picture of some real-life situation, the biblical truth remains an abstraction. Unless they see a video running in their minds, the biblical concept remains vague and unhelpful. The message has no apparent bearing on their lives until they visualize some person, event, or circumstance in their everyday world."[4]

In sermon application, we either straightforwardly explain or we demonstrate through real-to-life examples what effect we hope the sermon will have in listeners' lives.

Biblical Integrity

The desire to display relevance may tempt us to neglect biblical authority. Rather than beginning with the text, then offering applications appropriate to the biblical truth, we sometimes mistakenly begin with the applications we want to make and then find some text to which we can attach our applications. John Stott writes concerning preachers who yield to such temptation, "All their sermons are earthed in the real world, but where they come from (one is tempted to add) heaven alone knows. They certainly do not appear to come out of the Bible. On the contrary, these preachers have allowed the biblical revelation to slip through their fingers."[5]

Such neglect diminishes the effectiveness of our preaching for two reasons: the Bible is the sole authority for effective application, and listeners cannot escape application rooted in the Word.

The Bible Is the Sole Authority for Effective Application

Paul bid Timothy to "preach *the* Word" (2 Tim. 4:2, emphasis added). We preach God's Word, not our opinions, not pop psychology, not Lucado or Yancey or Warren. Though

---

4. Donald R. Sunukjian, *Invitation to Biblical Preaching: Proclaiming Truth with Clarity and Relevance* (Grand Rapids: Kregel, 2007), 106.
5. John Stott, *Between Two Worlds: The Art of Preaching in the Twentieth Century* (Grand Rapids: Eerdmans, 1982), 143.

these may aid our study, the Bible serves as the sole authority for effective preaching.

"God promises He will bless the church that teaches His Word," explains Bob Russell. "The Bible is compared to a seed that grows when it's planted, so we need to sow it. The Bible is compared to a sword that cuts, so we need to brandish it. The Bible is compared to food that nourishes, so we need to serve it up."[6]

Effective sermons grow from, build on, and submit to the Word of God. Likewise, effective sermon application grows from, builds on, and submits to the Word of God. Biblical preachers use the Word to correct, rebuke, and encourage (2 Tim. 4:2). They use the Word to equip listeners to live in a godly manner (2 Tim. 3:17). They use the Word to impart guidance (Ps. 119:130). They use the Word to offer comfort (Ps. 119:28).

A friend once told me about a sermon he heard while visiting a church in the western United States. At the time my friend was not a Christian, but he was searching, seeking to satisfy a gnawing spiritual hunger. He opened the Yellow Pages and chose a church at random, hoping to find spiritual guidance. When the preacher rose to deliver his "sermon," he opened his text—not the Bible, but the *Earthquake Preparedness Guide.*

I did not hear the sermon, but I can imagine the application: find your home's safest refuge, develop a disaster plan, practice it twice a year, and if all else fails, move east!

Is it wrong to explain what to do in the case of an earthquake? Certainly not. Did the "sermon" satisfy my friend's spiritual hunger? Absolutely not!

Whether or not they realize it, people sit in our pews because they hunger for God, His Word, and the application of

6. Bob Russell, "Application: The Key to Relevant Preaching," audiotape of workshop presented at the National Preaching Summit, Indianapolis, 2000 (Bridgeport, IL: Christian Audio Tapes, 2000).

His Word to their lives. When we send them away still hungry, we fail as preachers.

Listeners Cannot Escape Application Rooted in the Word

If we preach our own ideas, people can take them or leave them. Listeners can ignore our opinions and, quite possibly, fare better for doing so. But if we preach God's Word, empowered by the Spirit, listeners cannot escape the application.

Fred Craddock illustrated this principle by telling of Jesus' sermon in Nazareth, recorded in Luke 4:23–27. Jesus needed to confront His Jewish listeners' racist attitudes toward Gentiles. He could have just stated it as opinion, "Guys and gals, I really

How does your respect for the Scripture text influence how you develop sermon application?

Haddon Robinson: To develop application for a sermon, you begin with the biblical text. You don't start with, "How can I apply something?" or "How can I be really practical?" You have to start with the biblical text.

Then you ask, "OK, what are the practical applications of this text? Here's the biblical principle . . . so what?" Every idea has its own implications. Too many sermons deal with all the flowers (applications) but don't get at the root (truth).

Bob Russell: Fred Craddock said we need to stay in the Scripture long enough to find its application. We can't come with a preconceived idea, just brush by the text, then make the application we wanted to make all along.

Think about the wise men who sought Jesus. We apply by saying, "Wise people always seek Jesus." The wise men went home another way. Using the same approach, we could apply

think we need to let go of our prejudice toward these Gentiles. God loves them, too, you know."

After such an approach, listeners would've chatted in the parking lot after church. "Whatcha think of that sermon? Oh, I don't know, preacher must be from California or something—so liberal. Where you wanna go for lunch?"

Instead of an approach based on opinion, though, Jesus appealed to His listeners from the Word of God. "Back in Elijah's day, a famine swept across the land," Jesus reminded them (my paraphrase). "When God sent Elijah to somebody for help, did you notice that He did not send Elijah to a Jew? No, He sent Elijah to a widow from Zarephath—a Gentile. And when Elisha healed a leper, there were many Jewish lepers

with, "Wise people always go home another way." No, stay in that story; see what it's *really* about. Craddock says, "Look at Herod. Look at the staff extended, the staff of a king." And then Jesus, the real King, came.

Application without Scripture is shallow and hollow. It is the Scripture that gives depth and credibility to the application.

Vic Pentz: Some preachers have a tendency to just ignore the text and run straight to "practical" applications that will play well to the culture. In the excesses of the eighties it was blatantly, "God wants you rich." Now it's, "God gave these principles that will make you successful." Ultimately, these messages may gather crowds, but they don't build strong churches or do anything for discipleship.

I find that people are hungry for Bible. The cookies can be on a higher shelf today than in the past. People are hungry for the intellectual side of Christian thought and research. To them this makes the Bible more alive and accessible.

he could've healed. But God told Elisha to heal Naaman the Syrian—another Gentile."

Their response? They tried to toss Jesus off a cliff!

If Jesus had preached opinion, listeners could have dis-

> *Application with biblical integrity submits to the sermon text.*

missed it. But because Jesus rooted the application in the Word, they could not escape it.[7]

Effective sermon application requires biblical integrity because the Bible is our sole authority and because listeners cannot escape application rooted in the Word.

We began with an assumption: Effective preaching includes application that preserves biblical integrity while pursuing contemporary relevance. Thus far we have defined effective preaching, application, and biblical integrity. Next, we will define contemporary relevance.

Contemporary Relevance

While some preachers neglect biblical authority, others neglect the real-life struggles, questions, and needs of the people who sit before them. They devote themselves to in-depth study and exegesis (and rightfully so) but fail to uncover the relevance of Scripture for their listeners. "Such preachers," explains Calvin Miller, "have a kind of seminary drone they learned from their uninteresting professors in the M.Div. wonderland of tidy theology. They are not generally aware that their congregation is thinning year by year. I know some of these preachers who are killing their churches with the dagger of dull homiletics. . . . The difference between a dull lecturer and a glorious preacher is all in the application."[8]

---

7. Ibid. This paraphrase is based on an idea from Bob Russell, borrowed from Fred Craddock.

8. Miller, *Preaching*, 50.

Effective preachers explain and demonstrate how biblical teaching makes a difference in the contemporary world. They not only speak of biblical concepts, ideas, and truths, but they also aim this biblical teaching precisely at the needs of their listeners.

In the inaugural Yale Lectures on Preaching in 1872, Henry Ward Beecher compared his early efforts at preaching to his early efforts at hunting. He fired his gun but never hit anything. Many sermons, he explained, fire off in the same manner—there's a bang, maybe some smoke, but nothing falls.

Six years later R. W. Dale delivered the Yale lectures. He continued Beecher's imagery: "Mr. Beecher said that in the elaborate doctrinal part of Jonathan Edwards's sermons the great preacher was only getting his guns into position; but that in his 'applications' he opened fire on the enemy. There are too many of us, I am afraid, who take so much time getting our guns 'into position' that we have to finish without firing a shot."[9]

Effective preachers connect biblical truth with the questions, struggles, and needs of contemporary listeners. They recognize that we do not preach to the clouds. We do not preach to empty pews (at least we hope not!). We do not preach to a faceless mass. We preach to people—people banged up and confused by life, people who need to know how God's Word makes a difference.

When preachers communicate with contemporary relevance, they follow God's own example. God delivered His word to men and women through contemporary writers who addressed specific situations and spoke to the needs of contemporary people. Paul did not write lofty doctrine that never left the clouds, he wrote to the Ephesians, the Romans, and the Philippians to teach them how to live for God in their

---

9. Stott, *Between Two Worlds*, 250.

At what point in your sermon preparation do you begin considering your listeners?

Tom Long: Before you open your Bible on Monday morning, you bring to consciousness your context—your people. Application is already in the mix.

Leander Keck is right about this—preaching is a priestly move before it's a prophetic move. You come on behalf of the people to the Word of God, and you say, "We have needs, we have concerns, we have issues—here they are." The text engages in a dialogical relationship with these needs until finally there is a fusing of horizons and a claim is exerted on the preacher. The preacher then turns around and speaks the truth, the whole truth, and nothing but the truth to the people. It's an interactive process.

Bob Russell: I like how Warren Wiersbe explained that the Bible is first a picture where we see Jesus, next it becomes a mirror where we see ourselves, then it becomes a window through which we see others and others see Christ in us.

particular circumstances. Luke did not write a biography of Jesus to be shelved in the back corner of a musty library; he wrote theology about the Son of God whom his friend Theophilus needed to know. And, in God's greatest expression of communication with humanity, He entered the world in a specific time, place, culture, and family: "The Word became flesh and made his dwelling among us" (John 1:14). God took eternal, divine truth and put flesh on it. Biblical preachers do the same.

"In the final analysis," explains Haddon Robinson, "effective application does not rely on techniques. It is more a stance than a method. Life-changing preaching does not talk to the

With that in mind, I'll first spend time in the text (the picture). Then I'll ask, "How does this show up in my life?" (the mirror). If I have a struggle in this area, I'll bet someone else does too (the window).

For instance, when I was preaching in 1 Peter, I came across the text that says, "Abstain from the evil desires that war against your soul." Some say that when you become a Christian, you won't have any more evil desires. Is this my experience? No, those evil desires still war against my soul. How? Well, sometimes I'll get really mad, and I am tempted to lose my temper and swear. I don't do it, but there is that word that wants to come up from the locker room forty years ago. Sometimes when somebody else gets a lot of acclaim, I am tempted to get jealous and cut them down. Sometimes when I am surfing through TV and see a scantily clad girl, I am tempted to lust. Those evil desires war against my soul.

These applications began when I considered how the text applied to me. They showed up in the sermon because I recognize my listeners have the same struggles.

people about the Bible. Instead, it talks to the people about themselves—their questions, hurts, fears, and struggles—from the Bible. When we approach the sermon with that philosophy, flint strikes steel. The flint of someone's problem strikes the steel of the Word of God, and a spark emerges that can set that person on fire for God."[10]

We pray our preaching will, indeed, set our listeners on fire for God. Such effectiveness requires application with biblical integrity and contemporary relevance.

---

10. Haddon Robinson, "What Authority Does a Preacher Have Anymore?" in *Mastering Contemporary Preaching*, ed. Marshall Shelley (Portland, OR: Multnomah and Christianity Today, 1989), 65.

Our assumption: Effective preaching includes application that preserves biblical integrity while pursuing contemporary relevance. We can understand the key terms as follows:

1. *Effective preaching* spurs transformation.
2. *Sermon application* explains or demonstrates how biblical teaching should impact listeners' lives.
3. Application with *biblical integrity* submits to the sermon text.
4. Application with *contemporary relevance* relates biblical teaching to the life circumstances of modern listeners.

Now we understand the assumption. But is our assumption valid? As we will learn in chapter 2, not everyone agrees.

CHAPTER TWO

Cooperating with the Holy Spirit

I began work on this project with the assumption outlined in the previous chapter: Effective preaching includes application that preserves biblical integrity while pursuing contemporary relevance. I surmised that all preachers shared this assumption. But as I began digging through books and journal articles, and as I began sharing conversations with preachers about sermon application, I learned that not everyone agrees. The study and the conversations challenged my perspectives and, frankly, altered them.

While some take for granted the need for preachers to include application in their sermons, others worry that such applications interfere with the work of the Holy Spirit. This chapter will examine both sides of the argument. Is the Spirit responsible for sermon application, or does the preacher hold this responsibility?

Side One: Application Is the Holy Spirit's Responsibility

Some scholars would view a book about sermon application as unneeded at best and potentially heretical. This perspective builds from three suppositions: God deals with listeners' hearts when they encounter Him in the text; preachers who apply risk interfering with God's efforts; and preachers who apply hold a deficient view of biblical authority.

God Deals with Listeners' Hearts

These scholars explain that the preacher is responsible to herald the good news—to serve as a messenger of the King. Through this proclamation, the preacher leads his congregation into an encounter with the text. At that point, God takes over. Karl Barth emphasized that a biblical text is not a dead object to study and evaluate and then transport to a contemporary audience. Instead, in and of itself, the Bible offers a living and dynamic encounter with God. Preachers pull their listeners into an encounter with God in the text; through His Spirit He will then convict, encourage, comfort, and deal with listeners' hearts as He sees fit. "Two things call for emphasis," Barth taught. "First, God is the one who works, and second, we humans must try to point to what is said in Scripture. There is no third thing."[1]

I recall a particular member of the first congregation where I preached regularly. Chuck possessed extensive theological education and was deeply thoughtful and introspective. When I began as a twenty-two-year-old preacher fresh out of Bible college, he intimidated me.

When I preached, though, Chuck annoyed me. He would sit in the pew with his eyes fixed the entire time, not on me, but on his Bible. When I invited the congregation to follow along

---

1. Karl Barth, *Homiletics* (Louisville: Westminster/John Knox Press, 1991), 45.

as I read the Scripture text of my sermon, Chuck opened his Bible like everyone else. However, when I finished reading and began my attempts to explain, illustrate, and apply the text, he did not look up like the rest of the congregation. Chuck remained in the text—flipping pages, studying, considering the text's immediate context, its canonical context, and its theological implications.

He tuned me out and tuned God in. "Imagine the nerve," I thought. "He's going to miss my great story about George Washington's wooden teeth. He'll never understand this text or how it applies to his life if he misses the story about the teeth."

Imagine the naivety and arrogance—not his but mine. Only the Word of God, and not the word of the preacher, legitimately carries the description "living and active." God's Word, not our words, are "sharper than any doubled-edged sword." Only Scripture "penetrates even to dividing soul and spirit, joints and marrow; it judges the thoughts and attitudes of the heart" (Heb. 4:12).

Interfering with God

Barth questioned whether humans even have the capability to apply Scripture. He said that for a person to bridge biblical truth to contemporary life represents a "serious problem" that has "no solution." Regardless of what the preacher does, it is the listener's encounter with God in the text that leads to life change. In fact, if preachers attempt to make application, they may actually interfere with the encounter God intends to have with listeners.[2]

This argument deserves consideration. For example, imagine that a preacher prepares a sermon on the biblical teaching

---

2. Karl Barth cited in "Is Application Necessary in the Expository Sermon?" by Hershael York and Scott Blue, *Southern Baptist Journal of Theology*, Summer 1999, 70.

that we are to love our neighbors (Luke 10:27). God intends to use that text to perform a large, momentous work in the life of a listener—perhaps a career change or the restoration of a severely damaged relationship. The preacher makes application, however, that appears anemic in comparison. "Loving your neighbor means to mow his yard when he's on vacation," the preacher explains. "Or, if her dog gets loose, and you see it on the side of the road, you go and rescue your neighbor's lost dog." All the while God wants one listener to leave his lucrative medical practice and rescue lost souls in Uganda and another listener to offer forgiveness to her abusive father.

While mowing our neighbor's yard and rescuing a neighbor's lost dog represent valid endeavors, such trite application may interfere with God's desire to perform a more momentous work. In application we run the danger of asking too little. God may desire more of the listener than we dare to point out.

Deficient View of the Text

Others with hesitations concerning sermon application dislike the idea of having to bridge the Bible to life, feeling that this approach assumes that the ancient text is inadequate and must be "delivered." Charles Dennison writes, "Good preaching doesn't pull the Word into our world as if the Word were deficient in itself and in need of our applicatory skills. Instead good preaching testifies and declares to us that we have been pulled into the Word which has its own marvelous sufficiency."[3]

The preacher who is serious about biblical authority will give attention to such warnings. To approach a text as though it were irrelevant or deficient represents gross arrogance. It is like saying, "Thanks, God. You did your best. It was a valiant effort, but I'll take it from here."

---

3. Charles Dennison cited in "Is Application Necessary in the Expository Sermon?" 71.

Consider a typical sermon based on Jesus' encounter with the rich young ruler. "Sell everything you have and give to the poor," Jesus bid the man of great wealth (Luke 18:22). Jesus' demand of "everything" seems a little steep for today's disciples. So, we bridge the teaching to today's audience and in so doing lose the power of God's teaching. "For you," we tell our listeners, "this means that you should increase your giving, maybe from 3 percent to 4 percent of your income. When you pass a beggar on the street, drop fifty cents into his cup. Go home this afternoon and evaluate your stock portfolio to see if you could get a better return on your investments, which would allow you to give more to the church" (it never hurts to mention giving twice!).

Perhaps we would better honor the text if we left the story as the gospel writers present it, and simply ask, "What kind of God is this who asks such amazing things of His disciples? Following Christ is serious business. He demands our everything." Through the power of the text, the Spirit may then lead listeners to contemplate the story's enormous implications for their own hearts, decisions, and actions.

Sermon application risks heresy when we imply, "This is what God says, but since it doesn't apply to you, let me pick up where God left off." Any application that views the text as deficient borders on blasphemy.

In sum, those who believe the Holy Spirit is responsible for sermon application base this conclusion on three assumptions:

1. God deals with listeners' hearts when they encounter Him in the text.
2. When preachers attempt to apply a text, they risk interfering with God's intention to apply it.
3. Sermon application diminishes biblical authority because it views the text as deficient.

Side Two: Application Is the Preacher's Responsibility

Some scholars view application in a manner that directly contrasts the views presented above. These homileticians view application as indispensable to the preacher's task. They believe preachers are responsible not only to teach about a text but also to explain and demonstrate how that text should impact listeners' lives. This belief grows from four assumptions: preachers are called to apply a text just as they are called to explain it; faith often expresses itself in the ordinary; texts written in ancient contexts need to be bridged to the contemporary world; and listeners need help applying the texts to their lives.

What role does the Holy Spirit play in sermon application?

Will Willimon: Application is God's responsibility. As a preacher, you're to pray, "God take this sermon and apply it as it ought to be applied, 'cause I have no idea how it ought to be applied." I'm trying to proclaim the Word; I'm a herald.

Tom Long: When you consider all the various tasks of the Spirit that are taught in Scripture, you realize that the Spirit is not just a moment in the preaching process, such as when He facilitates application. Instead, He is infused throughout the whole thing.

In the middle of preaching a sermon, the Spirit might guide me in a different direction than what I had planned, even to a different application. Also, though, the Spirit was present when I worked through the Greek syntax and the commentaries. I agree with Fred Craddock—any doctrine of the Spirit that cuts down on our workload is probably a wrong doctrine.

Called to Apply

Homileticians in this second camp point out that most scholars permit the explanation of a text. So on what basis should preachers be allowed to make *explanation* but prohibited from making *application*? If preachers must rely solely on the Spirit for one, must they not rely solely on the Spirit for both? Furthermore, if they rely entirely on the Spirit for both, the logical conclusion would require that preachers limit themselves from anything beyond simply reading the Scripture text aloud for their congregations—any additional comments,

Vic Pentz: My mail and e-mail tell me that the Holy Spirit really does much more application than I give Him credit for. People will tell me stories, and I'll think, "That's amazing. That's what God said to that person from that text." In a sense the preacher simply hosts an event of the Spirit inside a person—the Spirit steps into a listener's inner sanctuary and does His work.

Will Willimon: One time in a Bible study with college students, I taught about Jesus and the rich young man. I just threw the story out there, then said to the students, "You're like this man; you're young and successful." Of course I was prepared to say, "Now, Jesus doesn't tell everybody to sell everything and give it to the poor. He just says it to one guy. Maybe this guy had a problem."

But before I could get to this application, the students said, "Boy, Jesus must've had a lot of faith in this guy. He disappointed Jesus, but how great to be asked to do something big. I'm waiting to be asked to do something big. I don't know if I'd have the guts to do it, but I might."

If we give application some room, Jesus may believe in people more than we do.

whether explanation or application, would infringe on the Spirit's territory.

"What biblical or moral principle makes exegesis the work of the preacher and application exclusive province of the Spirit?" ask Hershael York and Scott Blue. "More plausible is the belief that the Holy Spirit uses human means to accomplish both tasks involved in the exposition."[4] The Spirit uses preachers to apply a text in the same way He uses them to explain a text.

Warren Wiersbe says similarly, "Yes, the Word does impress itself on the heart, and the Holy Spirit does convict, but the Word needs a preacher, and the Spirit needs a voice, and therefore the sermon needs an application."[5]

After Nehemiah led the Israelites to rebuild the wall around Jerusalem, Ezra assembled the people to read the Word of God to them. To assist Ezra, the Levites "instructed the people in the Law while the people were standing there. They read from the Book of the Law of God, making it clear and giving the meaning so that the people could understand what was being read" (Neh. 8:7–8). Beyond simply reading the Word of God, they offered explanation. Then, based on their explanation, the Levites joined Ezra and Nehemiah in offering direct application: "This day is sacred to the LORD your God. Do not mourn or weep. . . . Go and enjoy choice food and sweet drinks" (Neh. 8:9–10).

The Levites read, explained, and applied the Word of God. God calls preachers today to do the same. *Jesus' & application*

Faith Expressed in the Ordinary

While scholars in the first camp fear that a preacher's trite attempts at application will interfere with God's more momentous work, scholars in this second camp emphasize that faith

---

4. Hershael York and Scott Blue, "Is Application Necessary in the Expository Sermon?" 72.

5. Warren Wiersbe, *The Dynamics of Preaching* (Grand Rapids: Baker, 1999), 78.

most often expresses itself in the ordinary moments of life. Therefore, sermons should address ordinary matters.

To return to a previous example, these scholars would say that a sermon based on the biblical teaching of love for our neighbors should include such "trivial" matters as mowing our neighbor's yard when he is on vacation, or helping a neighbor retrieve her lost dog. If a preacher focuses only on the momentous possibilities, listeners will miss much of the nitty-gritty, nuts and bolts of faith expressed in real life. "Great application is often lived out in the smaller details of life," Haddon Robinson explains. "So the fact that something seems small does not mean it's trivial."[6]

The Bible itself, these homileticians argue, displays God's concern for the smaller matters of life. From Old Testament laws about injured donkeys (Exod. 22:10–11), to Jesus' comfort for those who worry over their clothing (Matt. 6:28), to Paul's instructions about women's hairstyles in Ephesus (1 Tim. 2:9), the Bible demonstrates that weighty theology leads to a comprehensive faith that impacts both the momentous and the ordinary aspects of life. Biblical preaching, then, presents the same comprehensive perspective of faith.

Texts Need to Be Bridged

Scholars who believe the preacher holds responsibility for sermon application maintain that because the Scriptures were written in ancient contexts, texts indeed need to be bridged to the contemporary world.

John Stott based his preaching textbook, *Between Two Worlds,* on this bridge-building image. "Our task is to enable God's revealed truth to flow out of the Scriptures into the lives

---

6. From an interview conducted with Haddon Robinson at Gordon-Conwell Theological Seminary.

of the men and women of today," Stott explains.[7] He believes preaching should follow the pattern of Jesus' incarnation: "God condescended to our humanity, though without surrendering his deity. Our bridges too must be firmly anchored on both sides of the chasm, by refusing either to compromise the divine content of the message or to ignore the human context in which it has to be spoken."[8]

Scholars such as Stott explain that this does not diminish the authority of the Word but instead amplifies it. The Bible itself displays how God's great truths worked out in people's lives in the circumstances they faced. Part of the preacher's responsibility involves explaining how the same great truths might work out in the circumstances listeners face today. Fulfilling this responsibility requires a preacher to observe the truth that a particular text offered in its ancient context and then to bridge that timeless truth to a contemporary context.

"Preachers must translate what the text means," explains Bryan Chapell. "This is more than an exegetical task. We must make the meaning of the text concrete for contemporary people in contemporary situations. If we do not place the proclamation of gospel truth in a present world it will have no continuing meaning."[9]

Listeners Need Help Applying

Scholars who believe preachers are responsible for sermon application insist that listeners need someone to help them see how biblical teaching should impact their lives. They explain that if sermons remain abstract, faith will remain abstract. If sermons fail to describe life change, lives won't change.

---

7. John Stott, *Between Two Worlds: The Art of Preaching in the Twentieth Century* (Grand Rapids: Eerdmans, 1982), 138.

8. Ibid., 145.

9. Bryan Chapell, *Christ-Centered Preaching* (Grand Rapids: Baker, 1994), 204.

Don Sunukjian writes,

> In order for relevance to occur and godliness to form, it is the speaker who will have to make the applications. The listeners usually will not make them for themselves. I know this from my own experience when I'm on vacation and listening to another preacher. At the end of his message—when the music is playing, the congregation is dismissed, and people are trying to step past me to get to the aisle—if he hasn't given me some concrete pictures of how the truth bears on my life, I don't stay seated in my chair, blocking others, appealing to my wife, "Honey, let me have a few minutes alone. I want to think of how this applies to my life." No. I rise like the others, turn to my wife, and say, "You want to get hamburgers or pizza? You get the girls; I'll get the boys. I'll meet you at the car."
>
> So the next time you as a speaker find yourself saying, "May the Spirit of God apply this to your hearts," what you're really saying is, "I haven't the vaguest idea how it fits; maybe you'll think of something." But they won't.[10]

To recap, those who believe preachers hold responsibility for sermon application arrive at this conclusion based on these assumptions:

1. Preachers are called to apply a text in the same way that they are called to explain a text.
2. Though we do not want to interfere with God's momentous work in listeners' lives, faith most often expresses itself in ordinary moments.
3. Because the Scriptures were written in ancient contexts, they need to be bridged to the contemporary world.

---

10. Donald R. Sunukjian, *Invitation to Biblical Preaching: Proclaiming Truth with Clarity and Relevance* (Grand Rapids: Kregel, 2007), 111.

   4. Listeners need help to see how biblical teaching should
       impact their lives.

A Synthesis of Two Extremes

Few homileticians, including those quoted above, take either
of the two views to its extreme. Though some believe the Holy
Spirit holds primary responsibility for sermon application, few
leave their sermons entirely in the ancient "there and then."
Though others believe the preacher holds primary responsibility for sermon application, few deny that the Spirit plays (or
at least should be permitted to play) an intimate role in the
process.

   A synthesis exists between the extremes that gives proper
credence to both the preacher's and the Holy Spirit's roles in

What role does the preacher play in sermon application?

Haddon Robinson: If preaching is designed to change lives,
people need to know, "How is my life to change?" Just as we
do not assume that people understand all the teachings of the
Bible without someone to open it up to them, how could we
assume people can apply it to their lives unless we give them
some direction?

Tom Long: I think it's homiletical sin to end a sermon with an
abstract doctrinal claim such as, "Jesus calls us to pick up our
crosses and follow him daily." Suppose a couple of teenagers
in the balcony wanted to do that or the Millers in the third pew.
They were persuaded; what would it look like if they obeyed? If
we don't know what it would look like for those teenagers or for
the Millers, then we're not ready to preach. If we do know what
it looks like, then we need to tell them.

sermon application. The synthesis includes three elements: the involvement of the Spirit and the preacher, application driven by the Word and the Spirit, and application that offers possibilities rather than lists.

The Spirit and the Preacher

Effective sermon application requires the involvement of both the Holy Spirit and the preacher. It is not a case of either/or; it is a case of both/and.

Peter's sermon in Acts 2 provides an example. The chapter evidences the Spirit's work from its first few verses, where Luke describes the Spirit descending on Peter and the other disciples like "a violent wind . . . from heaven" (v. 2), leaving "what seemed to be tongues of fire" resting on each of them (v. 3). "All

Vic Pentz: When I was thinking ahead about this conversation, I asked myself, what is an example of a great application? When has a preacher done this correctly and in a way we can emulate?

I thought of C. S. Lewis's famous sermon, "The Weight of Glory," that he preached at Oxford. Lewis preaches this amazing, almost whimsical message that seems to have absolutely no application. He talks about how the Bible says we will one day shine like the stars in the morning. He discusses what glory means—luminosity—we're going to have this luminosity.

Then he says, "Now think for a moment. That person sitting next to you will one day be a creature who, if you saw them today as they will one day be, you would be tempted to fall down and worship them. Therefore, should we not treat them that way now?"

It's a great example of application. The biblical truth ran its course without any attempt to wrestle it down into something practical. The sermon just came to a point where its application fell like a ripe, shiny apple out of the theology.

of them were filled with the Holy Spirit" (v. 4). Empowered by the Spirit, Peter stood to preach.

Apparently, the Holy Spirit also worked in the hearts of Peter's listeners. Acts 2:37 says the listeners "were cut to the heart." Though the text uses the passive tense, the overall emphasis of Acts 2 leaves little doubt who did the convicting—the Holy Spirit. The Spirit empowered Peter, and the Spirit used Peter's sermon to convict the listeners.

However, the work of the Spirit did not absolve Peter of his responsibility to make application. In fact, the people asked for it. After the listeners were "cut to the heart," they "said to Peter and the other apostles, 'Brothers, what shall we do?'" (Acts 2:37).

Though the Spirit worked throughout the sermon, the listeners still needed Peter to describe what they needed to do in response to the truths he had preached. Peter responded with clear, direct application: "Repent and be baptized, every one of you, in the name of Jesus Christ for the forgiveness of your sins" (Acts 2:38).

Today's preachers can find empowerment in the same Holy Spirit described in Acts 2. And, the Spirit still works in listeners' hearts. Effective preachers, however, imagine their listeners begging for clear direction: "Preacher, what shall we do? We want to respond to what you've said, but how do we respond? What will it look like if I implement in my life what you've taught?"

Effective sermon application requires both the preacher and the Spirit.[11]

---

11. One might ask, if effective application depends on both the Spirit and the preacher, to what extent does each contribute? We have no way of knowing. In fact, it may vary from sermon to sermon and from person to person. Probably the Spirit contributes the greater share; however, we also contribute significantly. If, for example, effective application required a cumulative input of "10," on some Sundays the preacher may contribute "4" and the Holy Spirit may contribute "6." Other Sundays we may offer a feeble "1" and the Spirit a hefty "9." However it works out from week to week, God holds us responsible to give our best effort and then trust that the Spirit will combine His efforts with ours to accomplish whatever He intends to accomplish in listeners' lives.

Word and Spirit Driven

Though effective sermons include application, the application does not drive such sermons. Instead, effective sermons are driven by the Word and the Spirit—God's truth and God's power.

I once heard a sermon that outlined steps listeners might take to climb out of financial debt. The text? Luke 15—the parable of the prodigal son. The steps included such principles as: "Just as the prodigal son developed a plan to climb out of the pigpen, so should you develop a plan to climb out of debt. Just as the prodigal son immediately got up and began implementing his plan, so should you go home this afternoon and begin by developing a budget."

Granted, the application provided helpful advice. Countless church members swim neck-deep in debt. However, the sermon drastically missed the real power and meaning of the parable of the prodigal son—grace. God longs to welcome His rebellious children back home. In comparison, the advice to write out a budget proves embarrassingly trivial and untrue to the text.

This particular sermon missed the power of the parable because it was application driven, rather than Word and Spirit driven. The preacher apparently began with some things he wanted to say—steps concerning how to climb out of debt—then searched for a biblical text to which he could attach his application. He began with the application rather than with the text.

Instead, a sermon based on the parable of the prodigal son should begin with the grace-filled message of the parable. To make application, the preacher would ask, "How does this teaching impact the lives of my listeners?" The application would then deal with such weighty issues as repentance and salvation and (based on the elder brother in the parable) offering a warm welcome to other repentant sinners.

Effective sermons include application, but they are not application driven. They are driven by the Word and the Spirit.

Possibilities Rather Than Lists

Effective sermon application offers possibilities that enhance the work of the Spirit instead of lists that can interfere with the work of the Spirit.

We preachers enjoy our lists and steps: "Four things that will give you a vibrant prayer life," or "Three steps to becoming the husband God wants you to be." Such application can limit what the Spirit may want to do with a text in the heart of a listener. What if the Spirit had wanted the listener to implement a fifth "thing" into her prayer life? What if a husband needed to do something to improve his marriage that the preacher hadn't thought of?

Furthermore, when we offer only lists or steps, we may inadvertently imply to listeners, "These are the *only* ways this teaching applies to your life." And, perhaps even more damaging, we may tell listeners, "You can take these four easy steps into any circumstance, any life situation, any struggle, and they will solve everything."

This approach risks interfering with the complex, meticulous, mysterious work of the Spirit. It ignores the tensions of life. It trivializes the knotty business of real faith. And, in the end, such an approach often results in legalistic listeners who have reduced the enormity of Christianity to a few rules and steps.

Instead of lists that can interfere with the work of the Spirit, we can offer possibilities that enhance the work of the Spirit. We do this by showing our listeners how a biblical teaching might apply in various circumstances. Consider this example, which describes various ways God might call a husband to apply a significant biblical teaching.

Husbands, God wants you to love your wife like Christ loved the church. This might involve an expression as simple as massaging her feet tonight before you go to bed; it might involve changing careers because your wife

How might a preacher cooperate with the Spirit in applying a text to listeners' lives?

Haddon Robinson: I do my best, but the Spirit takes my efforts and makes application beyond what I'm capable of. I can seldom apply the text to all the people in my congregation. But I assume that if I apply it specifically to one group, the Spirit can then take that and help other people see how it applies to them. There are times when someone listens to a sermon, and the Spirit of God says to them, "That's for you."

Vic Pentz: In my own preaching, I went through a period of working so hard to be relevant, and engaging, and practical, that I just wore myself out. I did my dissertation, titled *Preaching to Effect Transformation*, right at the point when I needed to get recharged with a classic, high view of preaching, where the burden is on the Holy Spirit. The pastor can be fumbling and unskilled, yet the Spirit works through our efforts to speak to people.

Now I've come back to an in-between perspective. It seems to me that the Spirit and the preacher work hand in hand to make application.

Bob Russell: Sometimes we make preaching more complicated than we need to. We ought to analyze our craft, but the truth is that the Bible is God's Word, and the Holy Spirit works through the preaching of the Bible; and if we keep coming back to the Book and try to teach it and make it clear and apply it, it's amazing what God can do.

screamed through tears that you love your job more than you love her—and you realize she's right. It might mean doing the dishes every evening after dinner; it might mean retiring early to spend the next twenty years cleansing the bedsores on her disease-ridden body. In whatever circumstance you find yourself and your marriage, ask, "How can I love my wife as Christ loved the church?"

Contrast the application in the previous paragraph with a typical trite list: "Step one, massage her feet tonight before bed. Step two, put a sweet note in her jacket before she leaves for work on Monday. Step three . . ."

When we offer possibilities, as opposed to steps or lists, we leave room for the Spirit to work in listeners' hearts. We may never mention the specific way a particular believer should apply the passage; however, we will have given enough possibilities to spur thoughts and ideas in every listener, regardless of their life circumstances. When we open listeners' hearts to the conviction of the Spirit, the Spirit makes whatever particular application each listener needs.

Numerous preachers have experienced this phenomenon. A few days after a particular sermon, a congregation member comments, "What you said last Sunday about _____ was so helpful. I really needed to hear that." The preacher goes home thinking, "My sermon didn't even mention that!" What happened? The Spirit took the preacher's words and made the needed application.

This will happen most often, and most effectively, when sermon application offers possibilities rather than lists.

To review, homileticians can go to one of two extremes in regard to sermon application. Some grant the Holy Spirit exclusive responsibility for application, while others grant such responsibility to the preacher. A synthesis of the two extremes gives proper credence to both the preacher and the Spirit. The synthesis includes these elements:

1. Effective sermon application requires both the preacher and the Holy Spirit.
2. Effective sermons include application, but they are not application driven. They are driven by the Word and the Spirit.
3. Effective sermon application offers possibilities that enhance the work of the Spirit, instead of lists that can interfere with the work of the Spirit.

CHAPTER THREE

Sermon Application in the Bible

Though the Bible contains a collection of books, none of the sixty-six is a homiletics textbook. However, the Bible does offer principles for how we should handle the Word of God and several example sermons. Not all of these example sermons contain elements that would fit our definition of sermon application,[1] but many do.

From these principles and sermons, we can piece together a biblical perspective on sermon application.

Application in Biblical Texts

Biblical writers intended readers to apply what they read. James admonished his audience, "Do not merely listen to the word, and so deceive yourselves. Do what it says. Anyone who listens to the word but does not do what it says is like a man who looks at his face in a mirror and, after looking at himself, goes away and immediately forgets what he looks like. But the man who looks intently into the perfect law that gives freedom, and continues to do this, not forgetting what he has heard, but doing it—he will be blessed in what he does" (James 1:22–25).

---

1. As noted in chapter 1, sermon application explains or demonstrates how biblical teaching should impact the lives of contemporary listeners.

In Isaiah, God likens His truth to snow and rain—He intends the Word to accomplish specific purposes in the lives of those who hear it: "As the rain and the snow come down from heaven, and do not return to it without watering the earth and making it bud and flourish, so that it yields seed for the sower and bread for the eater, so is my word that goes out from my mouth: It will not return to me empty, but will accomplish what I desire and achieve the purpose for which I sent it" (Isa. 55:10–11).

Paul instructed Titus to "teach what is in accord with sound doctrine" (Titus 2:1). The words "in accord" imply something that fits with or properly goes along with the "sound doctrine." What is in accord with sound doctrine, according to Titus, is behavior that reflects the doctrine:

> Teach the older men to be temperate, worthy of respect, self-controlled, and sound in faith, in love and in endurance. Likewise, teach the older women to be reverent in the way they live, not to be slanderers or addicted to much wine, but to teach what is good. Then they can train the younger women to love their husbands and children, to be self-controlled and pure, to be busy at home, to be kind, and to be subject to their husbands, so that no one will malign the word of God. Similarly, encourage the young men to be self-controlled. (Titus 2:2–6)

In each of these three examples, the biblical writers rooted their applications in biblical truth. James said to act on the Word; Isaiah pictured God's truth as impacting listeners' lives; and Paul instructed Titus to make application based on sound doctrine.

Scholars have long observed this pattern of "indicative–imperative" found in the Scriptures. After providing theological truth, the biblical writers often help readers consider the implications of these truths in their lives. The pattern often follows this logical formula: Because *(indicative)* is true, we must *(imperative)*. For example:

> *Indicative*: "I am the LORD your God, who brought you out of Egypt, out of the land of slavery" (Exod. 20:2).
>
> *Imperative:* "You shall have no other gods before me" (Exod. 20:3; the remainder of the Ten Commandments also flow out of the indicative in 20:2).

> *Indicative:* "It is for freedom that Christ has set us free" (Gal. 5:1a).
>
> *Imperative:* "Stand firm, then, and do not let yourselves be burdened again by a yoke of slavery" (Gal. 5:1b).

> *Indicative:* "You died, and your life is now hidden with Christ in God. When Christ, who is your life, appears, then you will also appear with him in glory" (Col. 3:3–4).
>
> *Imperative:* "Put to death, therefore, whatever belongs to your earthly nature: sexual immorality, impurity, lust, evil desires and greed, which is idolatry" (Col. 3:5).

Some preachers neglect the indicatives and jump straight to the imperatives. Their sermons become lists of do's and don'ts. They preach the Ten Commandments, for example, without rooting these commands in the identity of God (I confess my own guilt on this one). Tragically, their listeners often reduce faith to imperatives and miss the gravity and magnificence of biblical truth.

Other preachers, however, focus only on the indicatives and neglect the imperatives. These preachers dispense much information, expounding on the finer points of historical and grammatical analysis to establish theological truths, without helping listeners understand the implications of these truths. Their listeners become bloated by knowledge and fail to experience the transformation that comes from applying that knowledge from day to day.

Either mistake—imperatives without indicatives or indicatives without imperatives—falls short of biblical teaching and example. We proclaim truth. We explore the implications of this truth. Hence, we preach.

To emphasize this point with beginning preaching students, I encourage them to check their sermon outlines to make certain they display a balance of past and present tense. Past tense usually implies an explanation of the biblical text ("Paul told the Ephesians," or, "Abraham left Ur"); present tense usually implies the revealing of timeless truths and their implications for contemporary life. Most sermons should intentionally weave the two tenses together, joining biblical truth with the contemporary implications of that truth.[2]

Consider, for example, the following sermon outline that remains entirely in the past tense:

Text: Genesis 22:1–19
Thesis: God tested Abraham

   I. God instructed Abraham to sacrifice his son Isaac.
     A. The command must have horrified Abraham.
     B. The command made no sense—God had promised Abraham numerous descendants, who would come through Isaac.

---

2. Some exceptions to this principle exist. In narrative preaching, for example, a preacher may choose to stay in the biblical story, in the past tense, for a more extended period of time. In most situations, however, sermons prove most effective when they alternate between the past tense (biblical explanation) and the present tense (application).

    C. Abraham saddled the donkey, gathered Isaac and two servants, and obeyed.

    D. When Isaac asked about the offering, Abraham replied that God would provide.

II. Abraham built an altar on the mountain.

    A. He bound Isaac and raised his knife to slay him.

    B. An angel called out and stopped Abraham.

    C. God provided a ram in the thicket to sacrifice instead.

III. Because of Abraham's obedience, God reiterated His promise to bless Abraham.

While this "sermon" offers helpful information—information that the preacher should include in the message—it falls short of effective preaching because it fails to explore the contemporary implications of Abraham's story. Frankly, we could more accurately define this outline as a lecture rather than a sermon. It offers information about the Bible but stops before relating the Bible to listeners. Why do we need to know about this incident? How does the story translate to life and faith today? What does the text promise that applies universally, to both Abraham and us? What encouragements apply universally? If a listener took this text seriously, how might it make a difference in his or her decisions, relationships, or service to the kingdom?

> *Truth has implications. Sermons, consequently, need applications.*

Consider, now, a different sermon outline based on the same text:

Text: Genesis 22:1–19

Thesis: Faith in God's provision enables extraordinary obedience.

I. God's commands sometimes sound preposterous.
   A. God called Abraham to sacrifice his only son—a horrific and illogical command (what about the promise of many descendants?).
   B. God often calls us to obedience beyond our emotions and logic.

II. Obedience in difficult circumstances hinges on faith.
   A. Abraham's faith had been built on a lifetime of companionship with God.
   B. Abraham saddled up the donkey and obeyed, telling Isaac, "The Lord will provide."
   C. When they arrived on the mountain, God stopped Abraham from sacrificing Isaac and provided a substitutionary ram in the thicket.
   D. We can obey even the most difficult of God's commands when we believe God's promise to provide, based on our past experience with Him.

III. Faith in God's provision enables extraordinary obedience.
   A. God reiterated His covenant with Abraham.
   B. God also made a covenant with us; ours also involves a substitutionary sacrifice.
   C. When we trust in God's provision, we can obey Him to the furthest reaches.

While the first outline stays entirely in the past tense, the second keeps one eye on the biblical world and the other eye on the contemporary world. Listeners to a sermon using the second outline learn the same information offered in the first outline; however, with the second outline they also consider the implications of the text in their own lives.

Truth has implications. Sermons, consequently, need applications.

Grace and Application

The section above discussed the precedent of "indicative–imperative" in biblical texts. Biblical writers often outlined theological truths and then discussed the implications of these truths for their readers' lives. To take this discussion one step further, we also should note that the biblical indicatives that lead to imperatives often concern God's grace. Paul's epistles, when viewed in relation to their overall flow and structure, provide the clearest examples of this.

Paul spends the first eleven chapters of Romans offering a detailed account of God's grace, brought to fruition on the cross. Having established the doctrine of grace, the letter then makes a clear turn toward application in 12:1: "Therefore, I urge you, brothers, in view of God's mercy, to offer your bodies as living sacrifices, holy and pleasing to God—this is your spiritual act of worship."[3] The remainder of the epistle demonstrates specific ways listeners can offer their bodies as living sacrifices in light of God's mercy, which Paul described in the first eleven chapters. These applications include using one's spiritual gifts to build up the body (12:3–8), loving one another (12:9–21), submitting to authorities (13:1–7), behaving decently (13:8–14), and limiting one's personal freedoms for the sake of mutual edification (14:1–15:13).

Paul's letter to the Colossians provides another example. The first two chapters describe the supremacy, sufficiency, and grace of Jesus Christ: "For God was pleased to have all his fullness dwell in him, and through him to reconcile to himself all things, whether things on earth or things in heaven,

---

3. The term translated "spiritual" in Romans 12:1 (NIV) translates vaguely into English. Other versions offer such translations as "reasonable" (KJV and NKJV), "sensible" (CEV), or "truly the way to" (NLT). In its Romans 12 context, the term implies that based on God's mercy, it simply makes sense for us to offer our bodies as living sacrifices. The indicative (God's mercy) serves as the natural catalyst of the imperative (offer ourselves).

When we turn our sermons toward contemporary life, how specific should we be?

Vic Pentz: Sometimes the text itself authorizes you to get more specific than at other times. Last Sunday I made some pretty specific applications. I was talking about David's anointing. I dealt with the Lord not looking upon man the way man does—the outward appearance. God looks upon the heart.

In the sermon, I said that we're exactly the same way, only primarily with women. The shift from the written word to the pictorial image in our culture has tyrannized women. When our grandmothers were in their teen years, they could pick up a Robert Browning poem and read, "My beloved has azure eyes," or "eyes like sapphire." A woman would look in the mirror and think, "I have blue eyes, I'm beautiful, I'm lovable." They were affirmed by the words of the poem. I said, "How many women today feel affirmed by the cover of Cosmopolitan magazine?"

This was a specific critique of the culture. I felt authorized by the specificity of the biblical text: "Don't look at the outward appearance."

by making peace through his blood, shed on the cross" (Col. 1:19–20). Colossians 3:1–3 turns the epistle toward application: "Since, then, you have been raised with Christ, set your hearts on things above, where Christ is seated at the right hand of God. Set your minds on things above, not on earthly things. For you died, and your life is now hidden with Christ in God." Paul turns more specific as he continues: "Put to death, therefore, whatever belongs to your earthly nature: sexual immorality, impurity, lust, evil desires and greed, which is idolatry" (Col. 3:5), and, "Clothe yourselves with compassion, kindness, humility, gentleness and patience" (Col. 3:12). The remainder of the letter makes application to godly households (3:18–4:1)

Bob Russell: Sometimes a particular circumstance calls for specific application. For example, a local Kroger displayed our church newspaper in front of their store until somebody complained that they were displaying religious materials. So they pulled our papers (of course, they kept displaying some pretty raunchy newspapers).

It made our people angry. Some responded to Kroger with not-so-Christlike e-mails and voice mails. It was an embarrassment to the church—a few people stepped over the line in the name of Jesus.

Soon thereafter I happened to be preaching about gentleness and about how Christians should respond to others. I said with a quiet voice, "You know, when you send angry e-mails and leave hateful voice mails for the manager of Kroger, it damages our witness as a church, and it causes the world to think less of the church and of Christians."

I don't get that specific very often, but certain circumstances call for it. We must ask ourselves what God would have us to say.

and readers' prayer lives (4:2–6) and then gives specific instructions concerning certain individuals (4:7–18).

Biblical preachers follow Paul's example of rooting application in grace. Though their sermons may include exhortations toward obedience, the sermons first point to the reason behind the obedience—we obey in gratitude for the grace we have received. Otherwise, preachers push their listeners toward legalism. "Exhortations for moral behavior apart from the work of the Savior degenerate into mere pharisaism," writes Bryan Chapell, "even if preachers advocate the actions with biblical evidence and good intent."[4]

---

4. Bryan Chapell, *Christ-Centered Preaching: Redeeming the Expository Sermon* (Grand Rapids: Baker, 1994), 268.

Tom Long agrees: "We move to moral application too quickly. We'll get a biblical text and describe it, then move immediately to, 'This is what you need to do.' We miss the intermediate step of, 'This is what God has done.' What we do reflects what God has done."[5] Long then offers this example:

> Not long ago a student of mine preached a sermon on Luke 7:36–50, in which Jesus eats in the home of Simon the Pharisee. A woman comes in and starts bathing Jesus with her hair and tears. This offends Simon. Jesus says to Simon, "Look at this woman." The preacher had an interesting insight, explaining that Simon had the woman stereotyped already. Jesus is saying, "Look at the woman."
>
> The preacher then, having made that point, moved instantly to, "I wonder how many people we're not really looking at." It's a great ethical point, but the text gives us the insight that *Jesus* really looked at the woman. He sees us and all of our sins and still loves us. This insight becomes the vision, the soil, the energy out of which we obey.[6]

To build from Dr. Long's classroom example, application based on Luke 7:36–50 might grow from a sense of grace as follows:

> The scandalous woman showered great affection on Jesus. She bathed His feet with perfume and tears and then wiped His feet with her hair. Simon didn't like it. He saw only a dirty, disreputable, disgusting sinner. How could Jesus—a supposed respected rabbi—allow such a woman to touch Him?
>
> The text says Jesus turned toward her, then said to Simon, "Do you see this woman?" (Luke 7:44).

---

5. From an interview conducted with Tom Long at Emory University in Atlanta, Georgia.

6. Ibid.

Note first that Jesus looked at the woman. While Simon saw a dirty, disreputable, disgusting sinner, Jesus saw a child of the Father, created in His own image. Jesus saw innocence that had been marred but could be recovered. Jesus saw a saint in the making. Jesus saw grace.

Aren't you glad Jesus has such vision? I share a great deal in common with that woman. My sins may not have been so public; however, they're just as disgusting. Yet Jesus looks at me not in disgust but in compassion. He sees in me a child of the Father, created in His image. He sees a saint in the making. He sees grace.

After Jesus looked at the woman, He invited Simon to do the same. Just as He invited Simon, Jesus bids us to view one another through His lenses of grace. Whom have I pierced with judgmental stares that I should welcome with eyes of grace? Imagine what a simple smile and nod of my head might mean to the homeless guy who hangs out at the gas station. Perhaps I could even buy him a candy bar and ask his name. Or maybe I could stop by and introduce myself to the ex-con my boss just hired and possibly invite him to lunch. How might things change if I viewed other people as Jesus views them—through lenses of grace?

Biblical application is rooted in grace.

What we bid our listeners to do should grow from what God has done.

Application and Biblical Preachers

Thus far we have learned that biblical writers included application in their texts. Let us now turn our attention toward the use of application by preachers in the Bible.

The following verses from 2 Timothy note specific ways the Bible should impact lives; then they couple application with the charge to preach: "All Scripture is God-breathed and is useful for teaching, rebuking, correcting and training in righteousness, so that the man of God may be thoroughly equipped for every good work. In the presence of God and of Christ Jesus, who will judge the living and the dead, and in view of his appearing and his kingdom, I give you this charge: Preach the Word; be prepared in season and out of season; correct, rebuke and encourage—with great patience and careful instruction" (2 Tim. 3:16–4:2).

The Bible, having its authority in God Himself, equips preachers to teach, rebuke, correct, and train (2 Tim. 3:16). Therefore, Paul exhorts Timothy to preach this Word in all seasons and, in his preaching, to correct, rebuke, and encourage (2 Tim. 4:2). Timothy was to preach God's Word and apply it.

When attempting to make application, what dangers should preachers guard against?

Will Willimon: Primarily, we should guard against writing anthropological sermons. In modern churches we tend to make sermons about ourselves, instead of about God. It takes heroic effort to be theological rather than anthropological these days.

I recall a sermon about the prodigal son in which the preacher said, "We draw from this story these principles for family life."

I thought, "You mean Jesus told this story to give helpful hints for families?" No, it's Christological. It's theological. It's about God.

Bob Russell: I was in a planning meeting with other preachers, and we were working on a sermon about Jesus walking

Jesus provided a significant example in His Sermon on the Mount, which contains a large amount of application. The sermon demonstrates a sharp focus on a central theme, "Unless your righteousness surpasses that of the Pharisees and the teachers of the law, you will certainly not enter the kingdom of heaven" (Matt. 5:20). Jesus offered a series of applications to explain how this teaching should impact specific aspects of His listeners' lives.

First, this teaching should result in healthier resolutions to interpersonal conflict (Matt. 5:21–26). While the Pharisees and teachers drew the proverbial line at murder, Jesus explained that people of surpassing righteousness deal with the root problem—anger. More specifically, such people will not offer gifts at the altar until they have reconciled with their brothers, and they will settle legal cases before they go to court.

---

on the water. The person making the proposal discussed the application: "We have to take risks, to get out of the boat like Peter did."

But the more we looked at that text, we decided that's not really what the text is about. While it does show Peter taking a risk, the passage is really about Jesus. Peter saw Jesus on the water and asked, "Who is it?" Jesus replied, "It is I." Jesus used the same language that God used in Exodus, "I am that I am."

The text isn't about taking a risk. At the end of an exhausting day of ministry, and in the midst of a frightening storm, Jesus reminded His disciples that they were living and ministering in the presence of God.

The application should build from this. Regardless what difficulties we face, we live and minister in the presence of God.

Second, this teaching should result in stronger marriages (Matt. 5:27–32). While the Pharisees and teachers prohibited adultery and required a certificate for divorce, Jesus explained that people of surpassing righteousness keep themselves pure from lust and do not divorce for any reason (except for marital unfaithfulness).

Jesus continued by making specific applications in regard to oath taking (Matt. 5:33–37), retribution (5:38–42), relationships with one's enemies (5:43–48), and acts of righteousness such as giving, prayer, and fasting (6:1–18).

Jesus taught that "unless your righteousness surpasses that of the Pharisees and the teachers of the law, you will cer-

How can we make certain that our applications maintain biblical integrity?

Tom Long: I don't know that we can be absolutely certain, but we can include certain safeguards in the homiletical process that will help.

Once we are confident of the parameters of our text—having examined various translations and the original language—we engage in a playful, creative process by asking a zillion questions of the text, until something happens. This results in a page full of insights. Then we do theological, historical, and literary analysis to test all of our insights.

As a part of this we read commentaries. The world of the larger church, as exemplified by commentaries and scholars, can tell us what the text *can't* mean. They can't provide the interpretation or the implications (only the preacher has one foot in his particular congregation and the other in the biblical text), but the commentaries can exercise a veto. They can say, for example, "Your application of the five porticos in the Gospel

tainly not enter the kingdom of heaven" (Matt. 5:20). Then, He applied that teaching to several specific life situations.

With the parable of the wise and foolish builders at the conclusion of the Sermon on the Mount, Jesus reinforced the need for His listeners to apply His teaching: "Therefore everyone who hears these words of mine and puts them into practice is like a wise man who built his house on the rock. . . . But everyone who hears these words of mine and does not put them into practice is like a foolish man who built his house on sand" (Matt. 7:24, 26).

We discover additional examples in the Old Testament. The Old Testament prophets displayed no hesitancy in including

of John as the five habits of highly successful people does not wash historically."

Haddon Robinson: One key, I believe, to making certain our applications remain in alignment with the text is to distinguish between necessary (if "A" is true, "B" *must be* true), probable, possible, improbable, and impossible implications.

Perhaps you're dealing with lying. It's a high, necessary implication to say it's wrong to cheat on your taxes. You're lying to the government—that's wrong. It can't be in the will of God. However, if somebody asks if you like their hat, do you have to be so committed to truth that you say, "That's the lousiest hat I've ever seen. I can't imagine somebody wearing it to work!"? That would be only a possible, or more likely an improbable, implication.

That kind of response may not be what the Bible was talking about when it said not to bear false witness. There are implications of truthfulness that I want to explore, but the purpose of that command was not to hurt people. It was to be honest, truthful, and thoughtful.

application in their preaching. They repeatedly explained how God's truths should impact the lives of their listeners. Based on the people's covenant relationship with God, the prophets spoke directly to their individual and national behavior.

- "Repent! Turn from your idols and renounce all your detestable practices!" (Ezek. 14:6).
- "Your hands are full of blood; wash and make yourselves clean. Take your evil deeds out of my sight! Stop doing wrong, learn to do right! Seek justice, encourage the oppressed. Defend the cause of the fatherless, plead the case of the widow" (Isa. 1:15–17).
- "Administer true justice; show mercy and compassion to one another. Do not oppress the widow or the fatherless, the alien or the poor. In your hearts do not think evil of each other" (Zech. 7:9–10).

The previous chapter of this book discussed Ezra's sermon in Nehemiah 8. This incident provides further insight for this chapter. After Nehemiah led the Israelites to rebuild the Jerusalem wall, Ezra the priest stood before the people and read the Book of the Law from daybreak until noon. In the midst of Ezra's reading, the Levites instructed the people and made the meaning of God's Word clear. After further reading on the second day, Ezra and the Levites gave application concerning the Feast of Booths: "Go out into the hill country and bring back branches from olive and wild olive trees, and from myrtles, palms and shade trees, to make booths" (Neh. 8:15).

Ezra and the Levites explained how the people should apply God's teaching, and the people immediately obeyed: "So the people went out and brought back branches and built themselves booths on their own roofs, in their courtyards, in the courts of the house of God and in the square by the Water Gate and the one by the Gate of Ephraim. The whole company that had returned from exile built booths and lived in them" (Neh. 8:16–17).

Further examples would only belabor the point: Preachers in the Bible frequently included application in their sermons.

We should consider what John Wesley once wrote in his journal, "This very day I heard many excellent truths delivered in the kirk. But as there was no application, it was likely to do as much good as the singing of a lark."[7]

> *Preachers in the Bible frequently included application in their sermons.*

Biblical Narrative *as* Application

Thus far, this chapter has discussed how biblical writers included application in their writing—often through a pattern of indicative–imperative, and often using indicatives that deal with God's grace. Further, the chapter has discussed how preachers in the Bible included application in their preaching.

Though the Bible includes numerous examples of application, some may argue that numerous biblical sermons and texts do not include application.

For example, some might point to the most often used biblical genre—narrative—and contend that narrative texts seldom make application. In His parables, Jesus frequently tells stories without offering any specific application. Similarly, Old Testament narratives often present the joys and struggles of God's people without indicating how such information should impact readers' lives. Adam sinned, Noah built, Abraham obeyed, Moses led, Joshua conquered, David ruled, Elijah prophesied, Daniel prayed, and Nehemiah rebuilt. And the reader is left asking, "So what?"

---

7. Warren Wiersbe, *The Dynamics of Preaching* (Grand Rapids: Baker, 1999), 77.

In response to this contention, we should consider this possibility: Perhaps such narratives are, themselves, application of theology. Recall again our definition: Sermon application explains or demonstrates how biblical teaching should impact the lives of contemporary listeners. In keeping with this definition, biblical narratives often *demonstrate* how theology impacted people's lives.

For instance, Genesis 6–7 could have stated a simple truth, "God remembers those who are faithful to Him." Instead, the chapters demonstrate how this truth worked out in Noah's life. The text does include the theological declaration (particularly in Gen. 8:1), but it couches the theology in application—a demonstration of the truth impacting life.

Likewise, Genesis 22 could have stated, "God provides for those who trust Him." Instead, the chapter demonstrates how this truth manifests itself in life circumstances. God commanded Abraham to sacrifice Isaac; He then provided a ram to take Isaac's place. Again, the text declares the theology (Gen. 22:8, 14), but it couches the truth in application.

The Bible teaches us to make application, provides examples of sermon application, and is itself, in cases such as the narratives above, application of theology.

We began in chapter 1 with an assumption: Effective sermons include application that preserves biblical integrity while pursuing contemporary relevance. Is the assumption valid? Though the answer proved more elusive than I originally and naïvely thought, it appears that we were on the right track.

However, we have much more to learn.

Illustratuns := Resources!
— Where do you get them?

CHAPTER FOUR

Avoiding Application Heresy

Haddon Robinson offers an illustration that gives an apt warning regarding application.

> Where my wife and I used to vacation in Colorado, there was a rope bridge that crossed a creek. In the Spring, when the snow was melting off the mountains, the creek would rage below—it was a frightening bridge to cross. Even so, we would watch as some people would just race across the bridge as though it were an easy footpath. Others, though, saw the potential danger, and proceeded slowly and carefully. Application is like a bridge, but it is filled with potential danger, so we must cross the bridge carefully.[1]

In my earliest sermons I had no fear of application: "Do this! Don't do that! Avoid these! Practice this!" I'd furrow my brow, raise my voice to a whine, wag my finger, and impetuously ramble through lists of directives. Those people needed to

---

1. Haddon Robinson, "The Preacher and the Message" class notes, Gordon-Conwell Theological Seminary, May 27, 2002.

be told what to do. And I needed to tell them. As I have grown, and hopefully matured at least a bit, I have learned to approach application more cautiously.

Like a naïve soldier who tears across a battlefield with reckless abandon, a foolish preacher tears into application. A wise preacher, like a seasoned soldier, has grown aware of potential land mines and proceeds cautiously.

The land mines represent application heresies that explode from pulpits when preachers put applications into God's mouth that neither He nor the human authors of His texts intended. This chapter will identify seven such land mines, and discuss how to avoid them in favor of applications that maintain biblical integrity.

Spiritualizing

Spiritualizing involves turning the physical realities of a biblical text into unwarranted spiritual analogies and applications. When preaching about Jesus calming the storm on Galilee, for example, a preacher might say, "This storm represents the storms that we often face on the sea of life." Or, when discussing the Israelites' seven-circuit march around the walls of Jericho, he might spiritualize the event by listing seven acts of obedience in response to which God will remove the obstacles that stand in our way. When preaching about God parting the Red Sea, he might spiritualize the text by saying, "The Red Sea represents the difficulties in your life. This text teaches that God will carve a path straight through them."

When we spiritualize the details of a text, we divorce that text from the original author's meaning and purpose. We snatch the authority from the inspired pen of the biblical writer and invest it in our own imaginations. Though the advice we give and applications we make may provide help to our listeners, we inadvertently put words into God's mouth that He never spoke.

We attach a "thus saith the Lord" to an application that would cause the original writer to scratch his head.

Details such as the storm, the walls of Jericho, and the Red Sea contribute to larger truths; we must not miss the forest while attempting to spiritualize the trees.

Furthermore, why would a preacher draw analogies from only one or two elements of the text and not from the rest of it? If the storm Jesus stilled represents our contemporary struggles, what does the boat represent? Or its stern? Or the cushion on which Jesus slept? Such arbitrary and subjective speculation could continue infinitely, pulling listeners farther and farther from the actual meaning and legitimate applications of the text.

A more extended and exaggerated example may further clarify this point. If we spiritualized the details of the parable of the Good Samaritan, the sermon might progress like this:

Text: "A man was going down from Jerusalem to Jericho."

Spiritualized Application: The man had a direction, a goal. You too should make plans in life. Sit down this afternoon and make a list of goals. Where will you be in five years or ten years? What will be your "Jericho"?

Text: "He fell into the hands of robbers."

Spiritualized Application: The robbers in your life may include your critics, your competitors, or even those voices of discouragement you heard years ago. These thieves want to steal your security, your optimism, and your joy. Don't let anyone steal your joy! Every morning, choose your attitude. Every morning, choose joy. Don't let those "robbers" get the best of you.

> *Text:* The Samaritan "put the man on his own donkey."
>
> *Spiritualized Application:* The donkey represents all animals that we might use in ministry. If you have a dog, you might take the dog to cheer up people in the nursing home. If you have sheep, you might offer a few to the church to use in next year's live nativity. If you have a horse, you might lend it to the Kiwanis Club so that they can give rides to underprivileged children at the fair.

Granted, it's an absurd example; however, it demonstrates the temptation to spiritualize details that contribute to a text's meaning. The spiritualized details send the preacher on distracting rabbit trails unauthorized by the text.

To avoid spiritualizing the details of a text, the preacher must determine what the original author intended to convey through the entire text. The parable of the Good Samaritan further clarifies Jesus' admonition to "love your neighbor as yourself" (Luke 10:27). A questioner, apparently hoping to justify his lack of love for certain kinds of people, asked, "And who is my neighbor?" (10:29). Jesus responded with the parable, which teaches that Jesus' followers should be neighbors to those in need. Jesus changed the focus from the recipient of the love to the character of the one who extends the love (cf. 10:29–36). Jesus calls His followers to *be* neighbors—to love sacrificially without limits or prejudice.

> *Spiritualizing involves turning the physical realities of a biblical text into unwarranted spiritual analogies and applications.*

To apply the teaching in a manner faithful to the text, the preacher would help listeners imagine to whom they can extend sacrificial love: "The single mom who lives two apartments

down from you? Her son who's in desperate need of male influence? Your cousin upstate who just lost his job? The family in
Haiti whose mud hut was flattened by a recent hurricane? To
whom has God called you to be a neighbor?"

Note that these applications flow from the overall teaching
of the parable, not from spiritualized details.

Moralizing

Moralizing is drawing moral exhortations from a text that
go beyond the text's intention. While spiritualizing—moralizing's cousin—finds distinction in its symbolic interpretation
of a text's physical realities, moralizing finds distinction in its
numerous demands, rules, and instructions. With moralistic
application, every text becomes an imperative; or, more often,
every text becomes a list of imperatives. The Bible certainly
contains a fair amount of moral and ethical instruction, and
as preachers we should faithfully preach these instructions. We
should reject the temptation to add to them, however.

One preacher, for example, presented a sermon based on
Aaron's priestly garb, described in Exodus 28. The application?
"Through this text God teaches that we need to dress up when
we come to church." One can almost imagine listeners' side-
way glances and judgmental glares toward the visitor wearing
a golf shirt.

We might moralize by offering instructions to parents
based on Eli's apparent failures with his sons, directives for
leaders based on David's kingship, or exhortations to take risks
based on Peter's willingness to get out of the boat and walk on
water. "Because he did, you should."

In each case we must ask ourselves: Did the original author
intend this text to imply these particular rules or instructions?
Does the Bible include the Eli story as helpful hints for dads,
the chronicles of David's kingship as leadership instructions

(which typically and ironically sound like principles taught in contemporary leadership books), or the narrative of Jesus' and Peter's stroll on the sea as an exhortation to take risks?

Similar to spiritualizing, the advice preachers offer in these cases to parents, leaders, or potential risk takers might include good ideas and suggestions. Do the particular texts, however, merit attaching the label "Thus saith the Lord" to the suggestions? Generally, no. We should recall Haddon Robinson's advice from the previous chapter, and distinguish between necessary, probable, possible, improbable, and impossible implications of a text. Moralizing often treats possible implications (good advice) as necessary implications (thus saith the Lord).

Again, an extended and exaggerated example may clarify the point. In a sermon based on Acts 3:1–12, a preacher might moralize the applications as follows:

Text: "A man crippled from birth was being carried to the temple gate."

Moralized Application: There are always people down on their luck who need a ride to church. This text teaches that you should seek out those people and give them rides.

Text: "Peter looked straight at" the lame man.

Moralized Application: When you see a beggar on the exit ramp, rather than refusing to make eye contact, you must give that beggar your full attention.

Text: "The people saw him walking and praising God. . . . They were filled with wonder."

Moralized Application: When you come to Christ, you must put your life change on display so that everyone around you will see the difference.

Text: "When Peter saw this," he began to preach.

> *Moralized Application:* You should always have a sermon in
> your back pocket, ready to deliver at a moment's
> notice.[2]

While these applications may offer good and even Christian advice, Acts 3:1–12 does not warrant a "thus saith the
Lord" for giving people rides to church. Instead, these verses
lay the basis for Peter's subsequent sermon by demonstrating
that beyond the physical assistance God calls His followers to
offer hurting people, the greatest gift that believers can offer
others is an encounter with Jesus Christ. "By faith in the name
of Jesus," Peter preached in the aftermath of the healing, "this
man whom you see and know was made strong. It is Jesus'
name and the faith that comes through him that has given this
complete healing to him" (Acts 3:16). Legitimate applications
would flow from this principle. While God certainly calls us to
offer physical assistance to the needy (multiple other Scriptures
attest to this), we also must take the next step and offer people
an encounter with Jesus. Applications
would then help people imagine what
this might look like for a food pantry ministry, perhaps, or for a nursing
home ministry.

*Moralizing draws
moral exhortations
from a text that go
beyond the text's
intention.*

Some listeners actually want their
preachers to pour endless streams of
regulations from the pulpit—a rule for every circumstance and
black-and-white instructions to clear up every gray area. Law
provides an easier standard than grace, and clarity feels more
secure than ambiguity. But preachers of the gospel must call
their listeners to standards higher than laws, lists, and morals.
They must equip their listeners with biblical principles that will

---

2. This example is expanded from one offered by Sidney Greidanus in *The
Modern Preacher and the Ancient Text: Interpreting and Preaching Biblical Literature* (Grand Rapids: Eerdmans, 1988), 164.

help them live in a Christian way, whatever the circumstances. "Our task is not to make people moral," explains Haddon Robinson; "our task is to help them think Christianly."[3]

Patternizing

Patternizing turns biblical descriptions of people or events into universally normative prescriptions for behavior. It turns descriptions into prescriptions, examples into mandates, and pictures into blueprints.

Preachers with a strong and legitimate desire to see the contemporary church reflect the ideals of the New Testament church (and I include myself in that category) face particular temptation to patternize. Indeed, Scripture offers principles concerning the believers' life, service, and ministry. Some Scriptures, however, simply narrate the stories of believers attempting to live out these principles. Or, as in the case of the epistles, some texts discuss how these principles apply to particular circumstances in particular cultures and time periods. Simply because a biblical narrative or epistle mentions something that happened or something that should happen in a particular circumstance does not necessarily imply that God intends the church of all times to emulate that practice.

Consider these examples, all from Acts:

- The apostles cast lots to choose a new leader (Acts 1:26). Does this simply describe their practice, or does it prescribe a universal pattern for choosing church leaders?
- Barnabas sold property and gave the money for the poor (Acts 4:37). Must all property owners follow suit?
- The disciples chose seven men with apparent Grecian background to care for the Grecian widows among them (Acts 6:3). Must all ministries to widows follow

---

3. Robinson, "The Preacher and the Message."

this design? Must the church delegate all acts of ministry to groups of seven, all of whom are male and have Grecian names?

Based on your observations, what mistakes do you believe preachers most often make related to sermon application?

Will Willimon: I think moralism just continues to be the downfall of us preachers. Once you lose the sense of the living Christ, it just degenerates into insufferable moralism.

We had a visiting preacher speak about the prodigal son. She did a good job of saying, "It ends in a party. They began to make merry. Wow, God is like that. He welcomes us degenerate, spoiled brats back home, and throws a party." Then she said, "Now, let me say to you students that this is not a license for neglecting your studies, or being irresponsible in your work, or taking chemical substances."

I thought, "Alright, yeah—they shouldn't neglect their studies or do those other things. But isn't it funny that Jesus had no inclination to say any of that in this text? Why should you say it if He didn't?"

Haddon Robinson: It's rape of the Bible to say in the name of God what God hasn't said. It's close to rape of the Bible to say to people, when the text doesn't warrant such a statement, "This is how you are to behave if you want to please God."

We have to be so careful about saying, "Thus saith the Lord." When that cat is out of the bag, we've put a definite binding on people. We must use this phrase carefully and only where the Bible does. A Bible college handbook has a rule about not wearing T-shirts to class, and they put a Bible verse next to it. When we put that verse there, we are implying "thus saith the Lord" when the Lord hasn't saith thus.

We intuitively recognize that God did not intend us to turn every biblical pattern, such as those above, into universally normative principles. Some patterns, though, we do intuitively apply as principles.

- The early church baptized new believers (Acts 2:38). Most churches today, in one form or another, follow this pattern.
- When believers gathered, they shared in the Lord's Supper (Acts 2:42). Churches today continue to celebrate the Lord's Supper.
- New Testament Christians placed special emphasis on gathering on the first day of the week (Acts 20:7). Churches throughout the centuries have gathered on Sunday.

Though few people, if any, follow the first list of examples, many do adhere to the second list. Clearly, the pattern alone does not necessitate a universal principle. By itself, a biblical example does not equal a divine mandate. We cannot turn every pattern into a principle. Such patternizing falls short of legitimate exegesis (and, therefore, legitimate sermon application) for three reasons: it ignores a text's intent, it ignores historical and cultural circumstances, and it forces an inconsistent hermeneutic.

Ignoring Intent

Patternizing ignores a text's intent. This common thread connects spiritualizing, moralizing, and patternizing. When Luke describes in Acts 1 how the apostles chose a new leader by casting lots, the text contains no indication that Luke intended for believers of all times to follow this pattern. No other text, in Acts or elsewhere, indicates such. Luke simply described what happened.

We must not confuse description with prescription. In the Old Testament, Leviticus prescribed precise practices for worship. Acts does not serve the same purpose for the New Testament. Leviticus was *prescriptive for* old covenant believers; Acts is *descriptive of* the first generation of new covenant believers. In Acts, Luke demonstrates through a series of narratives how God empowered the church to fulfill Christ's commission to be His witnesses "in Jerusalem, and in all Judea and Samaria, and to the ends of the earth" (Acts 1:8). Every scene in the Acts narrative contributes to this purpose. When we interpret Acts as a blueprint for modern church structure and practice, we divorce it from the text's intent, thereby leading to illegitimate applications.

Ignoring Circumstances

Second, patternizing falls short of legitimate exegesis because it ignores historical and cultural circumstances. Many (if not all) of the biblical books are occasional documents— they were "occasioned" by something that God inspired the biblical author to address. In the epistles, particularly, biblical writers confronted problems that had arisen in first-century churches or answered questions their leaders had raised by applying various elements of theology to the readers' particular circumstances. As we read these epistles, we eavesdrop on one side of the conversation.

We cannot assume that the application of an element of theology to a specific first-century occasion applies universally to the church of all locations and generations. Paul prohibited the women of Ephesus from braiding their hair (1 Tim. 2:9), for example, because something in Ephesus had occasioned such a prohibition. A woman in twenty-first century Kansas City need not worry about Paul's restriction on braids.

The same principle holds true outside the epistles. Jesus instructed His disciples to "wash one another's feet" because the practice demonstrated great humility in light of the dusty roads and open sandals of the day (John 13:14). When we patternize the instruction and literally wash one another's feet today, though the expression holds some significance, it does not hold the same significance that it held originally. We follow the intent of the instruction most faithfully through those acts of service that require the most humility in our culture— cleansing the bedsores of a nursing home patient, perhaps, or cleaning the apartment of the disabled person who lives down the street.

Forcing Inconsistency

Finally, patternizing falls short of legitimate exegesis because it forces an inconsistent hermeneutic. If we intended to follow the biblical pattern, consistency would require us to follow *all* of the patterns, rather than arbitrarily choosing some and discarding others. For example, in addition to dictating that we meet on the first day of the week to break bread (Acts 20:7), the same paragraph also must dictate that sermons go "on and on" until midnight (v. 7) so that someone falls asleep (v. 9a; this one we can probably handle!), tumbles out of the window to his death (v. 9b), and is raised back to life (v. 10). Conversation must then continue until daybreak (v. 11). All of this must take place in a house with three stories (v. 9) and in a room with many lamps (v. 8). If a preacher took the first part (meeting on the first day of the week to break bread) as a normative pattern, a consistent hermeneutic would require that he make the remainder of the pattern normative, as well.

If patternizing so easily leads to such downfalls, how, then, should preachers deal with examples and descriptive passages in the Bible? How do we interpret and apply the patterns without patternizing? To avoid the temptation, preachers must seek the principle behind the pattern. Rather than turning a pattern itself into a principle, they must recognize that specific examples simply reflect larger truths. Behind every pattern lies a principle. From every principle stems various patterns.

"For a biblical precedent to justify a present action," teaches Gordon Fee, "the principle of the action must be taught elsewhere."[4] To return to our previous discussion, the fact that Acts 20 describes the believers in Troas sharing in the Lord's Supper (v. 7) does not constitute a mandate for Christians today. Elsewhere in Scripture, however, Jesus commanded that His followers partake of the Lord's Supper to remember Him (1 Cor. 11:23–26). Acts 20 describes the believers in Troas fulfilling Jesus' command. Their example does not bind today's believers, but Jesus' command does.

Though the biblical example does not bind us, we should note that it certainly encourages us. Biblical examples have great value as they demonstrate the ups and downs and joys and heartaches of God's people attempting to live out biblical teaching. Their patterns put

Patternizing turns biblical descriptions of people or events into universally normative prescriptions for behavior.

flesh on principles, but they are not principles by themselves.

A sermon about the Lord's Supper from Acts 20, therefore, should connect the encouraging pattern (v. 7) to the binding principle (1 Cor. 11:23–26). Other miscellaneous details from Acts 20, such as the three-story house and the sermon that lasted until midnight, do not constitute universal mandates because the Bible does not present them as principles elsewhere.

---

4. Gordon Fee, *Gospel and Spirit: Issues in New Testament Hermeneutics* (Peabody, MA: Hendrickson, 1991), 95.

Biographical preaching presents a particular temptation to patternize. Because Abraham, Moses, or David acted a certain way or performed a certain task, preachers often assume that their listeners should too. This approach proves problematic, however, because some biblical characters' actions fly in the face of godly character. What we have learned about avoiding patternizing—seek the principle behind the pattern—certainly applies to biographical preaching.

"How do we discern God's will for our lives?" a preacher might ask. "Gideon provides an example." The preacher then encourages his listeners to "put out a fleece," as did Gideon

---

When you consider application for your own sermons, what is your greatest fear?

Vic Pentz: I fear that I might overapply to the extent that the sermon feels trivialized. The wonder, mystery, and the "otherness" of the text has been eviscerated by the sense that I have to make it easily digestible.

In the 1970s, when I came of age as a preacher, everything had to have a cash value—and most of it was very relational. A sermon might be titled, "Three Ways to Be a Good Dad," and they all begin with C.

The danger is that we turn everything into subjective, personalistic, platitudes that are not transformational. Or, they're no more transformational than Oprah or Dr. Phil. It must be bigger than that. Otherwise it's not worthy of this amazing thing that God has done in Jesus Christ.

Will Willimon: Preachers so often stand up and read some wonderful, crippling text and then say, "Now, I have three things I want to say. First . . ." You can almost feel the thing go limp. And you can already feel God evacuated.

(Judg. 6:36–40). Before offering such an application, however, the preacher should carefully consider whether or not Gideon's example finds a basis in a biblical principle taught elsewhere. Some scholars argue that Gideon actually disobeyed the principle, "Do not put the Lord your God to the test" (Matt. 4:7; see also Deut. 6:16), thereby providing a negative example that we should avoid emulating.

When we preach a descriptive text, we avoid patternizing by refraining from turning the example into a mandate and instead seeking the principle behind the pattern.

I heard a sermon about Jesus inviting people to work in the vineyard. The preacher said, "How do we work in the vineyard? Courtesy. When you're buying groceries, when's the last time you said 'Thank you' to the salesclerk for the work that she does?"

I'm sitting there thinking, "Jesus Christ died for *that*? Being nice to salesclerks?" We've just got to be careful with the gravity of the gospel.

Haddon Robinson: It's like what the Roman Catholic priest said about listening to confessions from nuns—it feels like being stoned to death by popcorn. Or, as Peter Marshall said, the church is like an army of deep-sea divers marching triumphantly to pull the plugs out of bathtubs. There are heavy applications needed to maintain the dignity of the gospel.

On the other hand, I would point out that great applications are often lived out in the smaller details of life. So the fact that something may seem small does not mean it's trivial. The difference is what drives the sermon—the applications, or the biblical concept? Application-driven sermons are trivial. But concept-driven sermons do business in great waters.

Trivializing

Trivializing involves offering applications that diminish the gravity and complexity of the gospel. Scripture contains enormous truths with mammoth implications; when preachers reduce these to clichés and trite suggestions, they cheapen the mystery and power of what God accomplished through Jesus Christ. If our listeners desired helpful hints for battling life's minor annoyances, they could simply visit the magazine rack at the local newsstand. Instead of visiting the newsstand, however, they come to church, hoping for an encounter with a transcendent God. Our listeners "want to bump into what the apostle called the 'mystery of godliness'" writes Calvin Miller. "Sermons that are only about the practical things of this world are often too bound by this world to help them. . . . People see great sermons as rooted in a transcendence that becomes their entry point into a better world."[5]

Jesus provides an example in Mark 8. Toward the end of this chapter, He demonstrates the rhythm of indicative–imperative that we discussed in chapter 3. Jesus outlines truth about Himself and then the implications of that truth for any who wish to follow Him. Note, first, the gravity of the truth: "He then began to teach them that the Son of Man must suffer many things and be rejected by the elders, chief priests and teachers of the law, and that he must be killed and after three days rise again" (Mark 8:31).

This truth lies at the center of Christianity. Our faith and hope hinge on the death and resurrection of Jesus Christ. How might this truth apply to the lives of Jesus' listeners? What implications might begin to maintain the gravity of the truth? Jesus Himself offers such application:

---

5. Calvin Miller, *Preaching: The Art of Narrative Exposition* (Grand Rapids: Baker, 2006), 56.

Then he called the crowd to him along with his disciples and said: "If anyone would come after me, he must deny himself and take up his cross and follow me. For whoever wants to save his life will lose it, but whoever loses his life for me and for the gospel will save it. What good is it for a man to gain the whole world, yet forfeit his soul? Or what can a man give in exchange for his soul? If anyone is ashamed of me and my words in this adulterous and sinful generation, the Son of Man will be ashamed of him when he comes in his Father's glory with the holy angels." (Mark 8:34–38)

The truth: Jesus would be killed but raised three days later.

The application: Following Jesus requires complete self-sacrifice.

The one who gave His life demands that we give ours. In their sermons preachers may be tempted to lessen the demands of the gospel with applications such as these: "What might your 'cross' be? How might God be calling you to deny yourself? Perhaps, for you, this will mean giving up your afternoon soap operas one day a week to volunteer for the church food pantry. Or, the next time you go to the baseball game, you might order only one hot dog instead of two and give the extra money to the homeless guy outside of the stadium. Sacrifice yourself; take up your cross."

As Dr. Willimon asked, "Jesus Christ died for *that*?" Surely Jesus' sacrifice demands more of us than one hour of television or a hot dog at the ballpark.

A few paragraphs later, Jesus' demand faces a test. A rich, law-abiding young man approaches Jesus and asks, "What must I do to inherit eternal life?" (Mark 10:17). As the conversation proceeds, the man's reliance on his wealth surfaces, and Jesus' previous demand of complete sacrifice resurfaces. But how would Jesus approach the matter? Would He maintain the high standard He previously set, or would He lessen that standard, saying, "You're on the right track, so just continue taking baby steps. Submit yourself partially now, then a little more tomorrow, and a little more the next day"?

Because the man apparently had held back his finances, Jesus commanded him, "Go, sell everything you have and give to the poor, and you will have treasure in heaven. Then come, follow me" (Mark 10:21b). Though we may imagine Jesus speaking these words in a hardened, matter-of-fact manner, Mark highlights Jesus' love for the man that precedes, and in fact spurs, the command, "Jesus looked at him and loved him" (Mark 10:21a).

Though Jesus loved the young man—rather *because* Jesus loved him—Jesus refused to lessen the magnitude of the sacrifice required to follow Him. Sadly, the man walked away.

Preachers who love their congregations will hold them to high standards. They will refuse to lessen the high calling of discipleship. They will honor the gravity of biblical truth with applications of equal gravity.

I have already confessed my temptation to succumb to various application heresies. On more than one occasion, I recall trivializing applications regarding tithing. I have long held the conviction that Christians should give a minimum of ten percent of our incomes to the Lord and His work. Granted, the literal ten percent was an Old Testament law, and such laws do not bind New Testament Christians. The New Testament, however, never lessened the level of commitment required of those who live under the grace of the cross. Grace calls us to a higher standard than did the law. Ten percent, then, should be the floor from which we build our generosity toward the Lord and His work.

Though I held this conviction, I trivialized it in my preaching. "God desires ten percent," I preached. "But I realize that may be difficult for some of you. So, first evaluate where your giving stands today. Perhaps, like the average American Christian, you give about two percent. Set a goal to increase one percent a year—give three percent next year, four the next. After a few years you will have arrived at God's desire for your giving."

Soon after preaching this, I heard another preacher liken this approach to a conversation we might have with a recovering bank robber: "You robbed ten banks last year. Ultimately, God doesn't want you to rob any banks. But, I realize, that may be a big step for you. So, set a goal that next year you will just rob nine and the next year, eight. Continue at this pace and after a few years you will have arrived at God's desire for your life."

If, as I believe, God desires a minimum of ten percent giving, why would I lessen this in my applications? In a more recent sermon, I attempted to maintain the gravity of generosity:

> If we follow the biblical teaching, we will not work our way toward a tithe. Instead, we will start with a tithe and work from there. Perhaps such generosity will be difficult in your present situation. If that is the case, you need to change your situation. Perhaps it will involve ridding yourself of a car payment, a cell phone bill, or a cable bill, or all three. Perhaps it will require downsizing your house and the accompanying payment. It may take some adjusting, but discipleship requires just that—a drastic adjustment, a complete sacrifice of all that we are and do.[6]

---

6. The application includes suggestions—possible implications—that may seem small, such as getting rid of a cable bill. However, I hope that though they are small, the ideas are not trivial because they suggest ways the larger implication might work itself out in listeners' lives.

In His own teaching, Jesus outlined implications that maintained the gravity of gospel truth, rather than applications that trivialized that truth. Wise preachers follow suit, recognizing that significant truth calls for significant application.

> *Trivializing involves offering applications that diminish the gravity and complexity of the gospel.*

Normalizing

Normalizing is implying that a biblical passage will apply in the same manner to every person, despite differing circumstances. Such an approach ignores the complexities of life and faith. It assumes that Christians all lead identical lives, face identical problems, and therefore need identical applications.

Scripture itself demonstrates different applications of the same truths. For example, one issue in the New Testament church centered on whether or not Gentile converts should undergo circumcision. The Old Testament law required circumcision; in fact, circumcision stood central to the identity of Jewish people. Gentiles, however, did not need to become Jews before they could become Christians; yet, an uncircumcised Gentile preacher may have difficulty gaining a hearing among Jews.

Paul approached the issue with an overriding truth: Christians should limit their freedom in Christ only when exercising that freedom would hinder their ministry efforts (see 1 Cor. 8:13; 9:19–23; Gal. 5:1–6).

This overarching principle was applied in entirely opposite ways with Timothy and with Titus. Because of their Gentile backgrounds, neither had been circumcised. Should they be? Paul chose to circumcise Timothy so that he could have a hearing among unbelieving Jews (Acts 16:1–5). Paul refused to have Titus circumcised, however, lest legalistic believers be allowed to inhibit other believers' freedom (Gal. 2:1–5). The same truth was applied to different circumstances in opposite ways. Often preachers neglect such complexities by normalizing their applications.

"Honor your father and your mother," the Bible teaches. How might this apply to listeners? Consider, for example, adult listeners whose parents have fallen into poor health. How might these adult children best honor their parents? A naïve preacher will offer one application: "You best honor your parents when you bring them into your own home to care for them. No other gesture will suffice; in fact, any other gesture is contrary to God's will and is therefore sin."

> *Normalizing is implying that a biblical passage will apply in the same manner to every person, despite differing circumstances.*

Such a broad stroke ignores the various circumstances in which listeners and their parents may find themselves. Sometimes adult children most honor their parents by allowing the parents to continue living in their own homes and by stopping by once a day to check on things or to care for them. Or, the most honoring gesture may involve financial assistance. In circumstances where the level or expertise of care needed goes beyond a child's ability, that adult child might best honor his or her parents through the hiring of a full-time nurse or by placing the parent in a nursing home.[7]

For adult children to bring ailing parents into their homes is indeed one way adult children may honor their parents. In other circumstances, however, other gestures may best fulfill the command to "honor your father and your mother." When we preach this principle to honor our parents, therefore,

7. This example is expanded from one provided by Haddon Robinson in "The Heresy of Application," in *The Art and Craft of Biblical Preaching: A Comprehensive Resource for Today's Communicators*, ed. Haddon Robinson and Craig Brian Larson (Grand Rapids: Zondervan, 2005), 309.

How can preachers make certain that their sermons apply to a variety of people who face a variety of circumstances?

Bob Russell: When we think about the application of a sermon, we need to move out of our own familiar environments and include the singles, the older people, the people from various backgrounds who face various difficulties.

When one of our associates, a young guy, preached about heaven, he mentioned that in heaven there will be no more anxious visits to the doctor's office and no more stillborn babies. I thought, "I wouldn't have considered those applications because I have healthy children."

The best way I can make certain to consider various listeners is to talk about my sermons with other people. If it's Wednesday or Thursday and you and I are going to lunch, I'll tell you about my upcoming sermon. I'll ask, "What do you think about this? How does it show up in your life?" I will listen and write something down that you say, and it will affect the applications I make in the sermon. If I'm with somebody who's interested in the arts, or who has a son or daughter going through a divorce, I'll hear them and it changes my perspective about how the text might apply to my various listeners.

Tom Long: I find it helpful, when I'm preaching in an environment where I know a number of the people, to think through who will be sitting in front of me. I see their faces and consider their circumstances. So-and-so just lost her husband. So-and-so is facing surgery this week. So-and-so's kid got rejected in college applications. I'll have all this swirling in my head as I develop the sermon and then watch and listen as the Bible starts speaking to the real issues of the people.

we will apply it most effectively by presenting, not a single, ironclad application, but various ways in which the passage might apply in various circumstances. This approach will help preachers avoid the heretical land mine of normalizing their applications.

Proof-texting

Proof-texting begins with an application and then uses various verses removed from their biblical contexts to support that application. Rather than allowing texts to speak for themselves, this approach uses the collection of texts as proof of an application the preacher conceived before he even opened the Bible. With this approach, preachers "treat the Bible as if it were a magical book or perhaps no more than an anthology of sayings for every occasion,"[8] all the while ignoring exegetical matters such as the literary context, historical circumstances, and the intent of the biblical authors.

Perhaps a preacher feels compelled to speak to the need for courageous leadership. Where might he find such an example? David was a leader. David showed great courage when he faced Goliath. Thus, he preaches a sermon from 1 Samuel 17 concerning courageous leadership. "Like David chose five smooth stones," he might say (note how quickly proof-texting leads to spiritualizing), "courageous leaders gather the five tools needed for effective leadership. As David refused Saul's armor, courageous leaders are willing to refuse the world's methods. Like David stood before Goliath . . ."

Where did the sermon begin? It began with the preacher's desire to speak about courageous leadership. The desire, though noble, led the preacher to a text on which he could force his preconceived ideas.

---

8. Walter C. Kaiser and Moises Silva, *An Introduction to Biblical Hermeneutics: The Search for Meaning* (Grand Rapids: Zondervan, 1994), 31.

Did the biblical author include the account of David facing Goliath as a mandate for courageous leadership, gathering the right leadership tools, and refusing the world's leadership methods? And (to cite other examples of proof-texting) did God include Ruth in the Bible to teach us how to be good in-laws? Did He include Nehemiah to help us raise funds for a new church gymnasium? Surely the biblical texts address larger themes and ideas.

A more legitimate reading of 1 Samuel 17, placed within the overall thought pattern of 1 Samuel, reveals God's providence, protection, and blessing on David, whom Samuel had anointed for kingship in the previous chapter. Legitimate applications would have less to do with gathering tools needed for effective leadership and more to do with God's providence.

Other examples of proof-texting surface when preachers use the Bible to justify beliefs they already hold. In the nineteenth century, for example, preachers on both sides of the slavery issue used the Bible to justify their stance. Today the same kind of proof-texting arises around issues such as homosexuality, abortion, women's roles in leadership, and miraculous gifts of the Spirit. In each instance, people on various sides of the issues rip assorted verses from their contexts and pile them together as evidence of their position.

Proof-texting begins with an application and then uses various verses removed from their biblical contexts to support that application.

A legitimate way exists, we should note, to begin with our ideas or questions and then consider what text(s) might address them. The legitimacy of this approach hinges on our allowing the texts to speak for themselves. We must put our original ideas on the shelf long enough to complete the necessary exegetical work that will determine the original meaning and justifiable contemporary applications of the texts. If the exegetical work reveals that our original idea had validity, then we can proceed in confidence. If the exegetical work reveals error in our original idea, however, we must bend our idea to the text, instead of bending the text to our idea.

When we proof-text, we proclaim our own thoughts, ideas, and positions as though they held divine authority. Instead of God's Word, we preach our words. Wise preachers allow the text to dictate the applications.

Promising the Unpromised

Promising the unpromised is guaranteeing listeners certain outcomes that biblical teaching does not truly assure.

Sometimes preachers draw promises from passages that contain no promises. Based on the David and Goliath narrative, which we discussed above, preachers have promised their congregations, "If you go out on a limb for God, if you take a risk for Him, this text promises that God will protect and bless you. So go home this week, go back to work, and take that risk. God will give you success." A listener who has considered a shaky business venture may take the preacher's words as God's Word and lose his life's savings. God will bless every risk we take? First Samuel 17 makes no such promise.

Preachers who give much attention to material blessings often quote 3 John 1:2 as though it offers a promise for all believers: "I wish above all things that thou mayest prosper and be in health" (KJV). These preachers proclaim, "God wants you to prosper, to enjoy wealth, to drive the Lexus instead of the Chevy. If you serve Him faithfully, such promises are yours to take hold of." In this text, however, John simply related his hope for his friend, Gaius. The text contains no promise of wealth (in fact the term the KJV translates as "prosper" does not necessarily imply financial prosperity) for Gaius or for believers today.

Of course, some passages do contain promises. But not all biblical promises apply in the same way to all people of all times. In some cases, God offered promises only to specific people or groups of people. God promised Abraham and Sarah a son (Gen. 17:16). That promise does not apply to all potential parents. Though God promised military victory to Old Testament Israel if they remained faithful (Deut. 20:4), that promise does not apply to every nation of every generation.

Additionally, some biblical promises find qualification in their context—either their immediate or the canonical context. For example, God promises to give whatever we ask for in prayer (Matt. 21:22). However, the immediate context qualifies the promise, making it dependent on the faith of the one praying (Matt. 21:21). In its canonical context, the promise finds qualification in our motives (James 4:3), purity (1 Peter 3:12), fellowship with God (John 15:7), and whether or not we pray according to God's will (1 John 5:14–15).

We have discussed several ways we might make promises to our listeners that God did not intend for today. Lest we wash away the sense that *any* promise applies to our listeners, let us recognize that the Bible contains numerous promises that do apply to our listeners. Though the specific aspects of the promises to Abraham and Israel do not apply to every one of all times, the larger principles do. God promises faithfulness to His children, for example, and He promises to reward those who remain faithful to Him. And though certain elements qualify God's promise to give whatever we ask for in prayer, the promise remains when these elements are in place.

Moreover, many promises hold universal application: "For God so loved the world that he gave his one and only Son, that whoever believes in him shall not perish but have eternal life" (John 3:16); "Everyone who calls on the name of the Lord will be saved" (Rom. 10:13); and, "Do not be anxious about anything, but in everything, by prayer and petition, with thanksgiving, present your requests to God. And the peace of God, which transcends all understanding, will guard your hearts and your minds in Christ Jesus" (Phil. 4:6–7).

Promising the unpromised is guaranteeing listeners certain outcomes that biblical teaching does not truly assure.

Enough promises apply to our listeners that we need not manipulate those promises that do not apply. A careful reading will reveal to the conscientious preacher what promises legitimately apply today.

Application land mines abound. The seven we have discussed hold the most immediate danger for preachers:

1. *Spiritualizing*: turning the physical realities of a biblical text into unwarranted spiritual analogies and applications.
2. *Moralizing*: drawing moral exhortations from a text that go beyond the text's intention.
3. *Patternizing*: turning biblical descriptions of people or events into universally normative prescriptions for behavior.
4. *Trivializing*: offering applications that diminish the gravity and complexity of the gospel.
5. *Normalizing*: implying that a biblical passage applies in the same manner to every person, despite differing circumstances.
6. *Proof-texting*: beginning with an application and then using various verses removed from their biblical contexts to support that application.
7. *Promising the Unpromised*: guaranteeing listeners certain outcomes that biblical teaching does not truly assure.

Being aware of these land mines, the seasoned preacher proceeds cautiously yet confidently toward sermon application that displays both biblical integrity and contemporary relevance.

But how does the preacher discover such application? We have outlined what land mines to avoid, but in what direction might the preacher proceed? In the next chapter we will begin developing a process that will lead the preacher to develop effective sermon application with biblical integrity.

CHAPTER FIVE

Developing Effective Sermon Application: Part 1

The first four chapters of this book offered a great deal of information about sermon application. In summary, the following points were made:

- Effective preaching includes application that preserves biblical integrity while pursuing contemporary relevance (chap. 1).
- Sermon application explains or demonstrates how biblical teaching should impact the lives of contemporary listeners (chap. 1).
- The preacher and the Holy Spirit cooperate to apply sermons to listeners' hearts and lives (chap. 2).
- The Bible teaches about and exemplifies effective sermon application (chap. 3).
- To preserve biblical integrity and pursue contemporary relevance, preachers must avoid seven application land mines (chap. 4).

We've gathered the pieces; now we can assemble the puzzle. This, of course, has been our goal all along—we began our journey hoping to develop a tool that will help us prepare sermon application with biblical integrity and contemporary relevance.

Imagine sitting in your office on a Monday morning. An open Bible lies on the desk next to a laptop computer. Commentaries and Bible dictionaries, open and strewn about, stare up at you. Yesterday's sermon has faded into a fuzzy memory; next Sunday looms. You hope to prepare an effective sermon—one that impacts listeners' lives. You have chosen your text. Last week's newsletter publicized the sermon's catchy title. Where should you begin?

In short, you should begin with the biblical text and then uncover its relevance for your listeners. Ten questions will lead you through this process. This chapter will discuss the first five; the next chapter will discuss the remaining five. Chapter 7 will then assemble the questions into a "Sermon Application Worksheet."

1. Biblical Teaching: What Did God Originally Teach Through This Text?

Our own creativity, intellect, or efforts cannot by themselves make an eternal impact on listeners' hearts. "The core value of preaching that changes lives," explains John Ortberg, "is that it's biblical. You and I don't change lives; God changes lives. For two thousand years, God has used the power of His Word to convict stubborn hearts of sin, to move cold spirits to repentance, and to lift faltering lives to hope."[1]

The first step toward developing effective sermon application, therefore, is to discover what truth, concept, or idea

---

1. John Ortberg, "Biblical Preaching Is About Life Change, Not Sermon Form," PreachingToday.com, http://www.preachingtoday.com/skills/style/2000 08.13.html (accessed June 26, 2008).

the sermon text teaches.[2] To discover what a text teaches, the preacher must discover what it originally taught. Gordon Fee and Douglas Stuart explain, "Biblical texts first of all *mean what they meant*. That is, we believe that God's Word for us today is first of all precisely what His Word was to them."[3] The applications of a text may vary from culture to culture, even listener to listener; however, the truths imbedded in God's Word—the truths we apply in sermons—do not change.

Discovering what God intended to teach the original readers through the original author requires proper exegesis of a text. Though an in-depth discussion of Bible exegesis lies beyond the purposes of this book, we should briefly note that proper exegesis includes observing the passage's literary and canonical context, clarifying any linguistic issues that arise within the text, researching the historical context, and examining others' interpretations (via commentaries and similar tools).[4] These efforts will enable the preacher to determine what God intended to teach the original readers through the original author, thus avoiding many of the application land mines discussed in the previous chapter.

The exegetical process will lead the preacher beyond the surface level details of the text, which often emerge at the initial

---

2. The remaining chapters will assume that a sermon grows from a single text of Scripture. However, the principles discussed will also apply to a more "topical" sermon that incorporates multiple texts. When using multiple texts, the preacher will have to consider what God intended to convey through the collection of texts being used. In these cases, however, the preacher should guard against proof-texting and instead allow each text to stand on its own, guarding against forcing the texts into a preconceived idea the preacher wants to convey.

3. Gordon Fee and Douglas Stuart, *How to Read the Bible for All Its Worth* (Grand Rapids: Zondervan, 1982), 13.

4. For help concerning Bible exegesis, readers might refer to Fee and Stuart, *How to Read the Bible for All Its Worth*; John Hayes and Carl Holladay, *Biblical Exegesis: A Beginner's Handbook* (Louisville: Westminster John Knox, 2007); Mal Couch, ed., *An Introduction to Classical Evangelical Hermeneutics* (Grand Rapids: Kregel, 2000); and Sidney Greidanus, *The Modern Preacher and the Ancient Text: Interpreting and Preaching Biblical Literature* (Grand Rapids: Eerdmans, 1988).

reading of the passage and tempt preachers to make naïve leaps toward superficial applications. Proper exegesis will enable the preacher to discern the larger picture to which the details contribute. This overall message of the text provides the basis for biblical application. Sidney Greidanus explains,

> One of the major pitfalls of application is that preachers transfer isolated elements of the text rather than its specific message. Although this practice creates the impression of relevance, it is only pseudo-relevance, for historically the relevance of the text inhered not in the separate elements but in the combination of elements as these formed the specific message which was proclaimed to the original hearers/readers. In order to retain that original relevance and authority, preachers ought to adhere to that original message also in their application.
>
> Concentration on the original message will keep the sermon from being sidetracked by all kinds of "practical" remarks that may be related to elements of the text but have nothing to do with the intended message. . . . Concentration on the original message is the only way toward valid application.[5]

Texts often include details that hold great significance, but they hold this significance only in relation to the larger message of the text. The details by themselves, divorced from the text's larger message, do not provide a valid basis for application. The fact that Paul began his evangelistic efforts in Philippi at a river outside the city gate (Acts 16:13), for example, does not necessitate that all evangelistic efforts begin at rivers. The river simply advances the narrative of Paul's encounter with Lydia, which exemplifies the early church's Spirit-empowered efforts

---

5. Greidanus, *The Modern Preacher and the Ancient Text*, 166.

to fulfill Jesus' Great Commission. The river holds significance only as it relates to this larger message.

The following diagrams[6] demonstrate how applying elements that make up a message differs from applying the message itself:

Applying Elements That Make Up the Message

Text Element 1   ⟶   Application 1

Text Element 2   ⟶   Application 2

Text Element 3   ⟶   Application 3

Applying the Message

   Text Element 1

+ Text Element 2

+ Text Element 3

= The Message   ⟶   Applications

Application with biblical integrity grows from the message of a text.

Concerning the primacy of the text's message in the sermon, Tom Long offers an additional insight worth remembering.

> I put this question to beginning students: "Could you have preached the sermon you preached without having encountered this particular biblical text?" With this question I don't let them get away with, for example, preaching 1 Corinthians 13 and doing a one-size-fits-all sermon on love. They could say, "Well I got love out of the text." Perhaps they did, but it was an accidental, thematic encounter.

---

6. Modified from diagrams by Greidanus (ibid., 167).

How can a preacher make certain not to lose the power of a text in the exegetical process?

Tom Long: Paul Riceour has a notion that we move from naivety, to objectification, then to a second naivety. In the first naivety, we say, "The Bible is the Word of God; it speaks God." Then, we objectify it when we say, "The Bible is an ancient document that speaks in a foreign language," and we dissect it. If the process freezes there, we've objectified biblical knowledge.

Ideally, though, the exegesis leads us to *recover* what is now a second naivety: The Bible is the Word of God; I understand it through the cultural, historical, and sociological contexts. Then it seizes me again with the same force it did originally.

The trouble with many commentaries is that they approach the text only from the standpoint of objectification, so you get processes but no theological power.

I want to know that you could not have said what you said without having encountered this particular biblical passage. I will ask students, "Can you point to something in this text that is persuasive exegetically that governed what you said in this sermon?"[7]

The biblical text governs biblical sermon application. Therefore, we begin the application process by discovering what God originally taught through the sermon text.

2. Original Purpose: How Did God Intend This Text to Affect Its Original Readers?

God not only intended biblical texts to relate a message to the original readers, but He also intended that message to accomplish something in them. Therefore, after determin-

---

7. From an interview conducted with Tom Long at Emory University.

Vic Pentz: We're tempted with our exegesis to smooth out all the wrinkles in a text, but it's the scandal and mystery of the gospel that's so exciting. The paradox is that these startling texts are the ones that most energize people. We lose that energy if we try to just smooth it all out.

Willimon is great at this. He loves to present the Bible in all its bloody, gnarly, alienness. Then he'll say, "Isn't this just weird? This is crazy."

Will Willimon: I think a sermon needs some gaps like that, some lack of development, because that's when God invades the pulpit. If a sermon is too well constructed and developed, it becomes an object of beauty to admire—"Wow, that was great. Let's go home"—and the power of God through the preaching is lost. We should keep some of the outrage there.

ing what God taught through a particular passage, preachers should ask what He intended to accomplish. Did God want the original readers to repent of sin or to display more joy? Did He want them to live in a more godly manner or to develop a new perspective? Did He intend them to think a new thought or to practice a new habit?

Some psalms, for example, intended to spur their original audiences into worship. Other psalms equip believers to voice prayers of lament. Through the epistles that bear Timothy's name, God encouraged the young preacher to persevere in his ministry at Ephesus. Through the epistles addressed to Corinth, God confronted immorality and divisiveness in the Corinthian believers and compelled them to repent and reform their behavior.

We ask this second question, "How did God intend this text to affect its original readers?" because, as Zan Holmes wrote, "The major task of the preacher is to enable the Word of God to *happen again* for the preacher and the congregation."[8]

David Buttrick concurs: "True 'biblical preaching' will want to be faithful not only to a message, but to an *intention*. The question, 'What is the passage trying to do?' may well mark the beginning of homiletical obedience."[9]

While considering the purpose of a text may send our contemporary homiletical minds rushing toward how-to applications—three steps to a stronger prayer life, perhaps, or four ways to witness to your neighbor about Christ—before considering such lists we should ask if God originally intended the text to offer three steps, four ways, or similar applications. Often, the original purpose has little to do with how-tos.

Duane Litfin illustrated this principle in an interview with PreachingToday.com.

> One of my students preached a how-to sermon from Mark on casting out demons. Afterward, I asked him the point of the passage. "Mark was teaching us that Jesus had power over evil and the occult," he said. When I asked him why he turned that into a how-to, he said, "I couldn't think how to apply the point."
>
> The student assumed a need to have a how-to application—three things to do on Monday. He missed the real need expressed in this passage. "How about if we apply it this way," I said: "'Let's all get down on our knees and worship Jesus.'"[10]

---

8. Zan Holmes, "Enable the Word to Happen Again," in *Power in the Pulpit: How America's Most Effective Black Preachers Prepare Their Sermons*, ed. Cloephus J. LaRue (Louisville: Westminster John Knox, 2002), 74.

9. Buttrick quoted in Tom Long, *The Witness of Preaching*, 2nd ed. (Louisville: Westminster John Knox, 2005), 85.

10. Duane Litfin, "Reach Deeper Than 'Felt Needs,'" PreachingToday.com, http://www.preachingtoday.com/skills/interpretationandapplication/200304.18.html (accessed June 26, 2008).

Texts most often intend to help readers see, know, and respond to God (and by association, God's people). Preachers should consider this original purpose because, as we will learn below, what God intends a text to accomplish today reflects what He intended it to accomplish originally.

How does your consciousness of an audience influence how you develop a sermon?

Haddon Robinson: If you invite an amateur to speak, he'll ask, "What do you want me to talk about?" If you invite a more seasoned speaker, his first question will be, "To whom will I be speaking?"

A consciousness of the listeners influences how you explain the text and how you apply it. This is the essence of application in preaching—to take a biblical truth and show people how that truth can work itself out in the ordinary lives in which listeners exist every day.

When I'm preparing a sermon, I'll take the main thrust of a passage and ask, "Why am I preaching this truth to these particular people?" This enables me to help listeners connect God's truth and the business of living.

Bob Russell: John Stott, in *Between Two Worlds,* hit the nail on the head. The preacher's job is to bridge the gap between the biblical world and the modern world. Believing this, I try to keep both the text and the audience in mind while I'm writing a sermon.

When we develop sermons this way, preaching comes to life, and listeners recognize the Bible coming to life. If, while they're listening to the sermon, they know the preacher will give applications that help them connect the text to their lives, they listen more eagerly to the study. If they know it's all going to be academic, on the other hand, they mentally check out.

3. Comparison of Audiences: How Do My Listeners Compare with the Original Readers?

After considering what God taught the original readers of a text (question 1) and then considering how He intended that teaching to affect its original readers (question 2), we transition our thoughts toward our listeners by asking how they compare with the text's original readers.

In relation to the teaching and purpose of the text, what do my listeners hold in common with the original readers? How do they differ? Making this comparison will reveal how precisely we can mirror the original purpose of the text in our sermon.

For example, a gathering of young Christian leaders would hold certain commonalities with Timothy, the original reader of 1 Timothy 4:12a: "Don't let anyone look down on you because you are young." Like Timothy, these listeners face the obstacles, struggles, and questions common for a young person attempting to serve as a church leader. Therefore, the application given to Timothy applies directly to these listeners: "Set an example for the believers in speech, in life, in love, in faith and in purity" (1 Tim. 4:12b).

On the other hand, a typical American church member holds little in common with Philemon, the Christian slave owner whose slave, Onesimus, stole from him and then ran away. While on the run, Onesimus crossed paths with Paul and converted to Christianity. Christian integrity would require Onesimus to return to his master, Philemon—a dangerous prospect under normal circumstances, because Philemon held legal right to execute his runaway slave. Paul, therefore, sent a letter with Onesimus bidding Philemon, "If you consider me a partner, welcome him as you would welcome me" (Philem. 17). Most likely, listeners today will never find themselves facing Philemon's dilemma.

In cases where contemporary listeners hold little in common with the original readers, the preacher must abstract a broader principle from the text and then apply that principle to situations contemporary listeners might face.

When teaching about Philemon, the preacher might abstract a principle concerning the role of forgiveness in true Christian fellowship: If a brother or sister wrongs us, God calls us to offer them the same grace we have received through Jesus Christ. Then, to apply this principle, the preacher would imagine situations contemporary listeners might encounter in which they would need to offer forgiveness to a brother or sister.

First Corinthians provides an additional example. The believers in Corinth faced a spiritual dilemma that today's listeners probably will never face. Some Corinthian believers felt free to eat meat that had previously been offered to idols, knowing that the meat held no spiritual significance. Other believers felt that eating such meat implied participation in pagan worship, a matter of gross sacrilege and blasphemy. In 1 Corinthians 8–10, Paul explained that though eating such meat was not wrong in itself, faithful Christians should limit their freedom (in this case eating meat) when exercising that freedom might cause other Christians, for whom Jesus died, to stumble (1 Cor. 8:9–13).

Few contemporary believers lose sleep over whether or not they should eat meat that has been offered to idols. Because the contemporary circumstances do not match the original circumstances, the preacher should step back and view both situations through broader lenses. Though they may not share all the specifics, the original and contemporary audiences will always hold certain commonalities. We must ask, then, what our contemporary audience holds in common with the original audience.

When preaching from 1 Corinthians 8–10, the preacher should recognize that while today's listeners do not face the dilemma of meat offered to idols, they face similar dilemmas— situations where exercising their Christian freedom might cause a brother or sister to stumble. At this point the original and contemporary audiences intersect.

To apply Paul's teaching to a contemporary audience, the preacher would abstract a principle from 1 Corinthians 8–10 that applies to today's listeners: When faced with situations where exercising their Christian freedom might cause a brother or sister to stumble (perhaps enjoying a glass of wine after dinner, or smoking a cigar), contemporary listeners learn from 1 Corinthians 8–10 to limit their freedom when exercising it would cause a Christian brother or sister to stumble.

Haddon Robinson offers an image that will help us visualize this process. The image pictures a ladder that looks like an uppercase *A*. He calls this "The Ladder of Abstraction." To bridge from the biblical world (the left foot of the *A*), to the contemporary world (the right foot of the *A*), the preacher must abstract the biblical teaching up to the point where the two worlds intersect (the cross-stroke of the *A*). Thus the biblical teaching is abstracted, bridged to the contemporary world, and then applied to the contemporary world.

If the biblical and contemporary situations are similar, the preacher can bring the teaching straight across. If the two situations are dissimilar, the preacher will have to "climb" the ladder until he discovers the point where the two situations intersect.

A diagram including a couple examples will clarify the ladder of abstraction.[11]

---

11. Haddon Robinson, "The Heresy of Application," *Leadership*, Fall 1997, 25. Used by permission of *Leadership* journal. www.leadershipjournal.net.

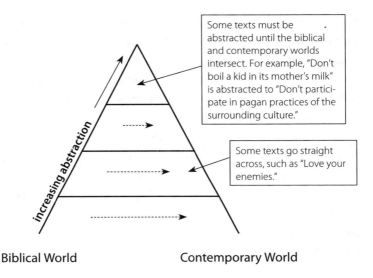

Some texts must be abstracted until the biblical and contemporary worlds intersect. For example, "Don't boil a kid in its mother's milk" is abstracted to "Don't participate in pagan practices of the surrounding culture."

Some texts go straight across, such as "Love your enemies."

Biblical World   Contemporary World

Robinson offers an additional tip to aid the preacher in using the ladder of abstraction: the original and contemporary situations will always hold two particular elements in common—the nature of God and the nature of humanity. Therefore, the preacher should first ask of a text, "What is the vision of God in this passage?" Robinson explains, "God is always there. Look for him. At different times he is the Creator, a good Father, the Redeemer, a rejected Lover, a Husband, a King, a Savior, a Warrior, a Judge, a Reaper, a vineyard Keeper, a banquet Host, a Fire, a Hen protecting her chicks, and so on."[12]

Second, the preacher should ask, "What in humanity rebels against that vision of God?" "The human factor," continues Robinson, "may show up in sins such as rebellion, unbelief, adultery, greed, laziness, selfishness, or gossip. It may also show up in people puzzling about the human condition as a result of sickness, grief, anxiety, doubt, trials, or the sense that

12. Haddon Robinson, *Biblical Preaching: The Development and Delivery of Expository Messages*, 2nd ed. (Grand Rapids: Baker, 2005), 94.

God has misplaced their names and addresses. It is this human factor that usually prompted the prophets and apostles to write what they did."[13]

This process will enable the preacher to bring the biblical message, written first to an ancient audience, to the contemporary audience with integrity.

We compare our listeners to the original readers to discern how precisely we can mirror the original purpose of the text. The more similar the two audiences, the more directly God's intention for the original readers applies to our listeners. The less similar the two audiences, the less direct the application. In such situations we abstract a broader principle that applies to our listeners.

4. Listener Need: What Listener Need Does This Text Address?

As long as we live in an imperfect world, listeners will sit before us with challenging needs burdening their hearts and minds. Unwise, ineffective preachers will ignore these needs. Such preachers expend great energy explaining Greek verb tenses, describing the various arguments of eschatological debate, and tracing the historical controversies concerning the doctrine of the Trinity, but fail to connect these matters to the needs of those who sit before them. They fail to consider the widow who worries that her Social Security check will not cover the rising cost of energy, or the middle-aged man considering an affair with a colleague at work, or the recent college graduate who struggles to find direction in life. The failure to acknowledge such needs communicates, at the very least, a lack of awareness; at worst it communicates a lack of concern.

---

13. Ibid., 95

The wise and effective preacher, on the other hand, "feels for the broken souls who come into the fellowship weeping inside, looking for any reason to feel they have a right to continue on in the world."[14] Such preachers recognize the value of relating biblical teaching to the needs and questions listeners carry with them into the church pews each Sunday. Their sermons turn yawning spectators into eager, involved listeners who lean forward, perk their ears, fix their eyes on the speaker, and begin imagining how the truth of God's Word might relate to the questions, concerns, and needs that burden them.

"Our task is to come to the text, to understand at a profound level what needs it's speaking to, and then help the listener get in touch with that need," explains Duane Litfin. Litfin teaches that we are not responsible for *creating* a need (as though preaching were a marketing ploy); instead, we bring to the surface the need that already exists. "It's almost a mistake to be asking, 'What are the felt needs of my audience?' and use those as my take-off point. As an expositor, I work the other way around. I come to the text, and I ask, 'What is the passage saying? What is the truth here? Why does God want us to know this? What is the need in our lives this is speaking to?"[15]

Because we exist as fallen people in a fallen world, our lives do not yet correspond entirely to biblical teaching. As the gap appears between our lives and a biblical teaching, a need surfaces. One key to effective sermon application, then, lies in addressing these needs. A preacher might ask concerning a sermon text, "What particular need does the text make apparent?" The following chart offers a few examples.

---

14. Calvin Miller, *Preaching: The Art of Narrative Exposition* (Grand Rapids: Baker, 2006), 52.
15. Litfin, "Reach Deeper Than 'Felt Needs,'" PreachingToday.com.

Biblical Teaching	Corresponding Need
Christian fellowship	Loneliness
God's grace	Guilt of sin
Sexual purity	Struggle with lust
God's sovereignty	Fear of the unknown
Faith	Doubt
God's guidance	Loss of direction

"The need element is to biblical truth what hunger is to food," teaches Wayne McDill.[16] The Word of God addresses the real-life struggles, questions, and needs of our listeners. Effective preachers uncover their listeners' hunger and then point them to the banquet table.

5. Sermon Purpose: What Should My Listeners Think, Feel, or Do Differently After Having Heard a Sermon from This Text?

A preacher I once knew wrote the words "So what?" in bold letters on a note card and then taped the note card to his desk in his office. The card reminded him, he explained, of his first homiletics teacher—a professor who concerned himself more with results than with tact. After a sweating, stuttering, first-year preaching student sat down after a feeble attempt at a sermon, this professor would jump from his seat and scream, "So what?! Why did I bother to come and hear that? What difference does it make in my life?" This teacher emphasized that sermons should do more than just convey information. Sermons should seek to accomplish something in listeners' lives.

Every Saturday evening the noted preacher A. W. Dale delivered the next day's sermon to his wife. One Saturday, after

16. Wayne McDill, *The 12 Essential Skills of Great Preaching* (Nashville: Broadman and Holman, 1994), 105.

As preachers consider their listeners, of what dangers should they be aware?

Will Willimon: We need to be careful that we don't give more attention to our listeners than we give to the text. Tom Long has said that the most momentous move in homiletics in our lifetime has been "the turn to the listener." We worry too much about rhetoric, strategy, technique, and analysis of the contemporary mind. I look around at the contemporary mind—it isn't all that impressive!

Tom Long: In *The Witness of Preaching,* I argue against "exegeting the congregation." One of my doctoral students wrote a dissertation taking the opposite stance (which I applaud), explaining how to go about exegeting a congregation. She was a seminary-trained pastor, ministering in a rural area, struggling to relate her preaching to the farmers in the community. To reach them, she needed to figure out how to understand their worldview.

I agree with her concept one hundred percent, but I disagree with the terminology. You "exegete" what is alien to you or distant from you. To exegete the congregation would be to say, "You're not who I am, and I have to do machinations in order to understand you."

Instead, I believe, a pastor should speak from an ethos of relationship, from their belonging to the people. Thus, the preacher isn't exegeting them but representing them.

Suppose I go to a passage that teaches about how Christians should respond to suffering. As a pastor, as a representative of the community, I brainstorm, "How have these people experienced suffering?" As their pastor, I'll know. And I can speak to their needs from the text. I haven't exegeted the congregation; I've represented them before the text.

he finished, Mrs. Dale asked her husband, "Tell me, why are you preaching that sermon?"[17]

The questions nag the diligent preacher: So what? Why will you preach that sermon? Until we answer such questions, we remain unprepared to preach. To preach effectively, we must define each sermon's purpose.

Furthermore, to apply effectively we also must define each sermon's purpose. Recall again our definition: Sermon application explains or demonstrates how biblical teaching should impact the lives of contemporary listeners. How can we explain or demonstrate how a teaching should affect our congregations if we have not asked, "How should this sermon impact my listeners?"

The sermon's purpose statement should reflect the original purpose of the sermon text. Recall the second and third questions above, "How did God intend this text to affect its original readers?" and "How do my listeners compare with the original readers?" The more closely our listeners compare to the original listeners (question 3), the more closely our sermon's purpose statement (question 5) reflects the original purpose of the text (question 2). Having answered these questions, the preacher may then develop a clear, concise, pregnant sentence that describes the intended impact of the sermon. "As a result of hearing this sermon," we might begin, "listeners should . . ."[18]

Tom Long teaches his students to complete this statement with "functions" that fall into one of three categories: cognitive, affective, or behavioral. "Sometimes I want my listeners

---

17. Robinson, *Biblical Preaching*, 106.

18. Note that the purpose statement focuses on the text and the listener, rather than on the sermon and the preacher. If it focused on the sermon and the preacher, it would be stated, "Through this sermon I will explain the four elements of faith," for example; or, "Through this sermon I will trace Abraham's journey to the Promised Land." Stating it in terms of the text and the listener forces the preacher to focus on the impact of the sermon rather than on the content of the sermon.

to think a new thought—perhaps to replace their old idea of stewardship with a new perspective of stewardship. Sometimes I want them to feel something different—maybe to have more joy than they had before hearing the sermon. Other times the sermon has a behavioral function—the sermon prepares the listeners to do something."[19]

Ultimately, to define the sermon's purpose statement we must ask: "What should my listeners think, feel, or do differently after having encountered this text?"

A few example purpose statements should prove helpful:

- As a result of hearing this sermon, listeners should examine their righteous acts to see if these acts grow from a spirit of love or a spirit of legalism.
- As a result of hearing this sermon, listeners should implement biblical steps to reconcile a hurting relationship.
- As a result of hearing this sermon, listeners should vow to live from this day forward in accordance with God's design for marriage.
- As a result of hearing this sermon, listeners should attempt at least one of three suggested ways to bolster their personal devotion to God.
- As a result of hearing this sermon, listeners should perceive prayer as a matter of relationship with God, rather than as a rigid routine.
- As a result of hearing this sermon, listeners should clarify their particular role in God's metanarrative.
- As a result of hearing this sermon, listeners should find more joy in service than they did previously.
- As a result of hearing this sermon, listeners should sense greater peace concerning their eternal inheritance than they did previously.

---

19. From an interview conducted with Tom Long at Emory University.

- As a result of hearing this sermon, listeners should humble themselves in worship, awestruck by God.

Beyond simply conveying information, an effective sermon seeks to accomplish a specific purpose. As the next chapter will reveal, this purpose relates closely with a sermon's application.

Before proceeding to the next chapter, however, let us review the first five questions by way of an example. Imagine you have begun preparing a sermon based on Job 38–42. Your exegetical work reveals that after Job experienced incredible heartache in the first two chapters of the book, he spent the next thirty-five chapters debating with his friends about God's apparent absence during the ordeal. Finally, in chapter 38, God speaks up. He points Job to creation, which people of the ancient world feared as mysterious, dark, and unknown. In essence, God says, "Job, take a look around. I created and sustain all you see (along with much you can't see). The sea and the storm stand at my beck and call. I made Leviathan my pet. And I managed to do it without your help. Job, *trust Me*." Job falls prostrate in repentant submission.

While preparing a sermon from Job 38–42, a preacher might make these notes as he walks through the first five questions:

1. *Biblical teaching*: What did God originally teach through this text?
   - God taught that He is sovereign over all of creation.

2. *Original purpose*: How did God intend this text to affect its original readers?
   - God intended the original readers to see creation as evidence that they could trust Him, even when they didn't understand why life had turned out as it had.

3. *Comparison of audiences*: How do my listeners compare with the original readers?

   • Though few of my listeners have faced tragedy to the extent of Job's, my listeners do sometimes find themselves wondering about the apparent absence of God during times of suffering.

4. *Listener need*: What listener need does this text address?

   • The text addresses the need to sense that something, or Someone, is in control and that life is more than just a series of random, haphazard, sometimes painful events.

5. *Sermon purpose*: What should my listeners think, feel, or do differently after having heard a sermon from this text?

   • After hearing this sermon, listeners should see creation itself as evidence that God is sovereign and trustworthy, even when life doesn't make sense.

CHAPTER SIX

Developing Effective Sermon Application: Part 2

Chapter 5 outlined the first five of ten questions that lead the preacher to sermon application with biblical integrity and contemporary relevance. This chapter will continue the discussion with questions 6 through 10.

6. Sermon Application: If the Sermon Accomplished Its Purpose in Specific Listeners Dealing with Specific Life Situations, How Might It Look?

This sixth question leads to the "nuts and bolts" of application. Once we have dealt with the text (questions 1 and 2), considered our listeners (questions 3 and 4), and defined the purpose of the sermon (question 5), we can begin imagining how listeners' lives might change if the sermon fulfilled its purpose in them.

To answer this question, the preacher progresses through three thoughts. First, the preacher reflects on the sermon's purpose statement (question 5). The purpose statement holds a close connection to the application, because it outlines what listeners should think, feel, or do differently after having heard the sermon. The application, then, pictures what it would look like for various listeners if they did, indeed, think, feel, or do differently.

Second, the preacher considers specific listeners. For example, assume a preacher defined the following purpose statement: "As a result of this sermon, listeners will watch for and celebrate what God is doing in and around them." After he determines this intention for the sermon, the preacher asks what it might look like if the sermon fulfilled its purpose in Les, the schoolteacher who sits in the third pew from the back; or in Brenda, the pediatrician who sings in the choir; or in Betty, the widow who arrives each Sunday in her blue dress. How might Les, Brenda, or Betty watch for and celebrate what God is doing in and around them?

Each week from 1945 until 1972, the *Arthur Godfrey Time* drew forty million radio listeners. When asked his secret, Godfrey explained that as he spoke into the microphone, instead of envisioning himself speaking to crowds of people in mysterious "Radioland," he imagined himself chatting with one individual—a truck driver rolling down the highway, a woman doing dishes in her kitchen, a patient lying in the hospital, or perhaps a lonely man or woman who thinks nobody cares. Godfrey's every word said to individuals, "I'm interested in you and I have something important to share."[1]

Often we think of our listeners only as a blur. Instead, imagine individual faces, expressions, smiles, and tears. Look into their eyes. We do not preach to an audience, we preach to Joe, the forty-seven-year-old mechanic who just sent his daughter to a private college more expensive than he can afford; and

---

1. Warren Wiersbe, *The Dynamics of Preaching* (Grand Rapids: Baker, 1999), 43.

Melissa, the twenty-seven-year-old accountant who lies awake at night regretting the abortion she had eleven years ago; and Brett, the fifty-year-old computer programmer whose boss pressures him toward unethical software usage; and Donna, the thirty-nine-year-old mother sandwiched between her pregnant teenage daughter and her increasingly confused elderly father.

Perhaps, to make certain he considers individuals, the preacher leafs through the church pictorial directory. He sees faces and remembers conversations. He recalls counseling sessions, weddings, births, and time shared in hospital waiting rooms. Or, he might imagine a cross section of listeners sitting around his desk as he prepares the sermon. He hears their questions, struggles, fears, and joys. He sees the looks in their eyes when they encounter God's truth in the biblical text. He dreams with them concerning the implications of the text in their everyday lives.

A little girl went with her mother to hear Charles Spurgeon preach. After listening for fifteen minutes, the girl whispered to her mother, "Mother, is Mr. Spurgeon speaking to *me*?" He was, as well as to the five thousand others.[2] Listeners will say the same of any preacher who speaks with individuals in mind.

Third, after considering specific individuals, the preacher considers the specific life circumstances these individual listeners face. What situation might Les the schoolteacher, Brenda the pediatrician, or Brett the computer programmer encounter where they need the lessons, encouragements, or tools offered in the sermon text? This question forces the preacher to consider how the truths of the text truly impact the day-to-day business of living. It transforms the application from broad generalities ("You need to be a more godly man") to specific images that reflect the tensions and struggles listeners face from the moment the Monday morning alarm begins blaring

---

2. Ibid., 42.

("Let us imagine how a godly father balances his blossoming accounting career with his kids' weekend soccer games, the praise band he plays in at church, and his wife's frustration that their marriage seems to have taken a backseat").

Instead of making generic application about death, consider the anguish of parents whose seventeen-year-old daughter is killed by a drunk driver; or of a soon-to-be widow struggling at the bedside of her cancer-ridden husband of sixty years. Instead of thinking generally about divorce, consider John and Mary, who are thinking about giving up after sixteen years and three kids. How might this sermon impact listeners who face these circumstances?

Don Sunukjian encourages preachers, once they have discovered the truth of a text, to "run the truth through an expanding grid of the various groups and life circumstances that are in your audience."[3] To develop this grid, the preacher begins thinking in large categories of people and life situations and then continues breaking down the large categories into specific details until a mental picture emerges.

For example, he may begin by considering how a biblical truth applies to a man (large category). To get more specific, he may think of a married man. For even greater specificity, he considers a married man who is in his second marriage and whose children struggle to accept their stepmother.

Or he may consider a woman. The woman lost her husband of twenty years to a car accident. She now raises three teenage children by herself. She senses her children beginning to rebel.

To add a third person to the grid, he might think of a single man. He owns a marketing firm that has struggled in

---

    3. Donald R. Sunukjian, *An Invitation to Biblical Preaching: Proclaiming Truth with Clarity and Relevance* (Grand Rapids: Kregel, 2007), 113.

an economic downturn. He might have to lay off a couple of employees—employees who are like his family.

Once we develop this grid, Sunukjian teaches, we sift the text's teaching through it. How do the truths imbedded in this sermon text apply to the people we've imagined? We think in specifics, visualizing circumstances, conversations, and confrontations. Then, in the sermon, we describe the pictures we've imagined.

For a more extended example, consider a sermon that grows from one of Jesus' beatitudes, "Blessed are those who are persecuted because of righteousness, for theirs is the kingdom of heaven" (Matt. 5:10). In the development of a mental grid, the preacher has imagined a wealthy, generous widow whose children oppose her generosity. How does Matthew 5:10 impact her specific situation? The sermon might include the following paragraphs:

> A widow finds great joy in generosity. Few things in life satisfy her heart like dipping into her mutual funds to help finance a new wing of a children's hospital, to support missionaries in Haiti, or to assist her church's new building project. Her grown children, though . . . well, they don't share the same generous spirit. With each check, each gesture, they see their inheritance dwindling.
>
> She meant to keep her latest gift secret. She gave significant support to an inner-city mission. The mission's appreciative and gushing director, though, couldn't keep quiet. So the widow's kids found out. She dreads the weekly brunch they'll share.
>
> "Mother, they're just taking advantage of you," her kids will say (again). "You've got to stop being fooled by these people. If you keep wasting our—rather, *your*

money, there'll be nothing left to live on later. You're just being foolish, mother. Foolish!"

She knows she's doing the right thing—God blessed her, and He expects her to bless others. So, she just smiles, accepts their barbs, changes the subject, and keeps on giving.

How can she endure her children's mockery? Well, she knows the promises of Jesus. She knows heaven awaits the faithful. And she intends to be faithful, regardless of the cost. When her children spew their disrespect, she holds her chin up and imagines the day when she'll hear, "Well done, my good and faithful giver."[4]

The power of sermon application grows from its detailed images. When listeners see pictures in their imaginations, they envision God's truth working itself out in their own lives.

Before we move to our seventh question, I feel compelled to offer one additional thought concerning the sixth question. While we consider how our sermon text applies to individuals personally, we also should consider how it applies to them on a community, relational level.

While placing the finishing touches on this book, I began work on another project that surveys biblical teaching concerning community dynamics among God's people.[5] Researching for that project forced me to rethink some aspects of this one. I grow increasingly convicted of our tendency as preachers to interpret texts through the individualistic lenses of contemporary culture, rather than through the corporate lenses of biblical cultures. Too often what the Bible presents as plural ("we" and "us"), we interpret in the singular ("I" and "me").

---

4. This example grows from one offered by Sunukjian (ibid., 119).

5. Daniel Overdorf, *Rediscovering Purposeful Community: What the Bible Says About the Church* (Joplin, MO: College Press, 2010).

For example, I recently preached a sermon based on Paul's metaphors of the church in 1 Corinthians 3. The church functions like a field, Paul taught—while human leaders plant and water, only God holds the power to bring growth. Also, the church functions like a building, constructed on the foundation of Jesus Christ Himself.

I struggled to develop applications. In the midst of this struggle, I realized I had thought only of how the text might apply to individuals personally. How can God bring about growth in each individual listener? How can my listeners make Jesus the foundation of their own lives?

While such questions remain valid and might find answers in other texts, this particular text in 1 Corinthians 3 offered metaphors of the church community. The application, then, needed to address the community implications of the metaphors. If a church depended on God for growth, and if a community built itself on the foundation of Jesus Christ, what might it look like?

I decided to package the application in three questions. After explaining the text and the metaphors, I asked: "In our church, what do we talk about most? What are we most known for? Where do we first turn our attention?" With these questions, I invited listeners to envision our church if we talked most about Christ, if others most knew us for our exaltation of Christ, and if any sense of crisis or celebration sent us first and foremost to Christ. In keeping with this sixth question ("What would it look like if the sermon accomplished its purpose in specific listeners facing specific life situations?"), I described how individuals within the church body might live out the applications, but each individual description served only as a brushstroke to help paint the picture of the church community.

Many passages, though applicable to individuals, do not apply only to individuals personally, as though faith manifests itself only between the individual and God. Instead, many texts apply to individuals as they function within the church community.

The six questions above lead the preacher to sermon application with biblical integrity and contemporary relevance. Before inserting such application into a sermon manuscript, however, the preacher should sift the application through four safeguards.

How can we make certain our applications hold relevance for people's lives?

Tom Long: I've been having an argument in my mind, brought on by Henry Nouwen's book *Creative Ministry*. He criticizes the preacher who begins a sermon by saying, "Life is so pressed by calendars and clocks and pressure, and we're crowding God out of our lives." Nouwen says, "That may be true of the preacher, but think of the woman on the back pew who spent her week on a park bench throwing popcorn to the squirrels. The preacher missed her."

Yes, she was there. But so were the people overburdened by schedules and commitments.

Week after week, it seems to me, we aim for different targets. Based on our understanding of the text and of our congregation, each Sunday we have different people in mind to whom the text will most relate. Everyone will hear the sermon, but some will connect more closely to it than others.

Part of our responsibility, then, based primarily on pastoral art, is to keep rolling through the Rolodex of the congregation in our minds and considering who the text wants to speak to.

Bob Russell: I feel we should make certain that most of our applications relate to Monday, not Sunday. As preachers, our

7. Safeguard: Does This Application Exalt God?

Though we previously discussed the importance of defining particular purpose statements for each sermon, all sermons should seek the highest purpose of glorifying God. We hold as our ultimate aim, always, to exalt Christ. We must make certain, then, that our applications never diminish the glory of God or cause listeners to think less of Him.

lives center around the business of the church, so our inclination is to make applications such as, "You need to volunteer to teach a class. You need to tithe. You need to attend church services."

I want people to sense that biblical truth applies not only within the church building, but also [to] their relationships with their coworkers, how they treat the little leaguers that they coach, and the decisions they make concerning their aging parents.

Vic Pentz: I find that people, more and more, want help unpacking what is going on in the culture. People sense that something is wrong, but they can't quite put their finger on it. We can assist them by equipping them with a Christian worldview. This is how they will find the most relevance in our sermons. Rather than just telling people how to behave, it's far more exciting—for our listeners and for us—to build a thought world in a community of believers.

The great preachers of the past did this, and they set the intellectual pace for the culture—John Wesley, John Calvin, and Martin Luther. We need more preachers like that today, people like John Stott, who can take on secularism, materialism, and pluralism with such skill that Christians can be proud of them.

Preachers most often diminish His glory when they emphasize one aspect of His nature to the neglect of His full nature, turning God into a one-dimensional caricature.

For example, in a sermon emphasizing God's power and authority, a preacher might say, "God is in charge. God holds all power and dominance. When you approach Him, then, you'd better come in holy fear. Because of who He is, you should be shakin' in your boots. You should approach God with the same trepidation with which you'd approach Hitler." The basic point has validity—acknowledgement of God's power should bring a holy fear and a humble approach before His throne. To compare God to Hitler, however, places an upsetting image in listener's minds that falls far short of glorifying Him. This caricature of God ignores other, critical aspects of His nature, such as God's love, kindness, and accessibility through the grace of Christ.

Conversely, in a sermon emphasizing God's love, kindness, and accessibility, a preacher might say, "God can't wait to hear from you. He's like your fishing buddy—He just enjoys hanging out with you. Or, He's like Santa Claus—God gets a twinkle in His eye every time you come to mind. All He wants is for you to be happy. So, you can come to Him just as you are and ask Him for whatever you want." Again, the basic point has validity—God does love us and relishes the relationship He shares with His children. To compare Him to a fishing buddy, however, or to Santa Claus, ignores God's holiness and majesty. While He has given His children access to His throne through Christ and warmly invites us to approach, if we approach Him as we approach our fishing buddy, we have missed the full extent of His nature.

Instead of these one-dimensional caricatures, application that exalts God invites listeners to approach God, but to approach Him in humility. He is King, but He is a benevolent King. He allows us access to His presence, but this allowance cost the blood of Christ to remove our guilt. We approach in holy fear but with confidence in the grace of Christ. We exalt God by inviting listeners to respond to God in His fullness.

8. Safeguard: Is This Application Consistent with the Text's Teaching and Purpose?

The first six questions lead the preacher to develop application that remains consistent with the text's teaching and purpose. Achieving such consistency holds enough importance, however, that after he outlines the sermon's application, the wise preacher will double-check. He will make certain that during the course of sermon preparation, of brainstorming and thinking creatively of how to reach a contemporary audience, he has not lost sight of the message of the text.

The preacher might ask himself how the original author would respond if he sat in the audience and heard the text applied. Would the author say "Amen!" or run to the front with arms waving, shouting "No, no—that's not at all what I meant!"? If the preacher surmises that the original author would find the text unrecognizable in the hazy mist of its applications, the preacher should return to the first question of the worksheet and give the application another try.

I recently had lunch with a friend who serves in local church ministry. Over hamburgers, we talked about writing sermons and preaching. "What do you do," he asked with a smile, "when you practice your sermon on Saturday and you realize that it just doesn't click?" Instead of giving an answer to his dilemma, as a more intelligent homiletics professor might, I further complicated the issue with another question: "What do you do when you practice your sermon on Saturday, and you realize it isn't biblical?"

We can prevent such moments of panic by incorporating this safeguard—question eight on the Sermon Application Worksheet—into our sermon preparation.

Sometimes we feel tempted to start with an application, then attach it to a text. Is this approach ever legitimate?

Vic Pentz: A while back I decided to preach a series concerning faith in the workplace. In one sermon, I wanted to talk about holding on to your integrity when everybody else is losing theirs. So, in a sense, I had the application before I had the text.

I began to think about what texts might legitimately speak to that issue. I settled on Daniel 1. The key, however, was that when I got to Daniel, I had to release the text to say what it says, without shoehorning it into a predetermined set of applications.

It was quite an adventure. I called it, "When Not to be a Team Player." I talked about Nebuchadnezzar's ethnic cleansing—trying to rid the boys of their Jewishness and school them in the ways of the Babylonians. The text says Daniel and the others excelled in their studies. I applied this by saying, "In your organization, even if it's a godless organization, work hard. Gain their respect. They may laugh at your faith, but when they're

9. Safeguard: Will This Application Motivate and Equip Listeners to Respond to the Text?

Whether sermon application involves explanation ("Our text this morning should lead each of us to reexamine our financial priorities") or demonstration (a story about someone who made financial changes to reflect biblical principles), it should motivate and equip listeners to respond.

David Mains tells of his conversation with a woman about a sermon she heard the previous Sunday. The message grew from Peter's sermon in Acts 2. Mains asked the woman, "What response was called for?"

"We were challenged to be a bold witness for Christ," she responded.

"Do you know how to do that?"

looking for someone to do a presentation, they might say, 'She may be a Christian, but she really does her homework.'" The application came straight from the text.

Later in the sermon I talked about how Daniel, instead of just disobeying the instructions about the royal food and wine, said, "Let's work something out." He didn't send an angry e-mail to the whole organization or picket outside the front door; he talked with his superiors and offered them another option. I applied this by saying, "When your boss asks you to do something that compromises your integrity, instead of just getting mad or leaving angry voicemails or e-mails, sit down and talk to her or him about it. Offer other options, other ways of handling the situation that will allow you to be a good worker and a good Christian."

For the whole sermon, I began with an idea of the application, but then I had to allow the text to speak for itself. Through my study I had the joy and thrill of discovering the application in a way that had integrity.

"I haven't a clue!"[6]

If a preacher challenges listeners to think, feel, or do something differently than they have before, he should present that application in a way that motivates and equips them to make the suggested changes. If he calls listeners to be bold witnesses, for example, he should provide help, ideas, suggestions, or real-to-life demonstrations that enable them to witness boldly.

David Veerman, an editor of the *Life Application Study Bible*, suggests that application should answer two questions for the listener: "So what?" and "Now what?" These questions force the preacher to progress beyond simply conveying facts and information and to assist listeners in recognizing (1) the

---

6. David Mains, "Killer Applications," *Leadership*, Spring 2004, 43–44.

relevance of the text for contemporary life and (2) how they can respond to the text.

Veerman offers as an example Luke 5:12–15, which tells of Jesus healing a leper. A sermon on this text might describe the horrors of leprosy in Jesus' day (information), and it should draw parallels to people today who face similar hardship (relevance). Application will take the next step, however, by challenging listeners to consider what "untouchables" they can touch for Christ and how exactly they can touch them.[7]

As previous chapters discussed, this suggestion does not imply that every sermon should contain a list of how-tos. In fact, a well-told example will itself equip listeners with motivation and ideas (overheard through the example) for making the suggested changes.

For instance, on one occasion I preached concerning Jesus' admonition to serve as "the light of the world," such that others "may see your good deeds and praise your Father in heaven" (Matt. 5:14–16). When Christians live out their faith in the daily routine, I explained, people of the world take notice. I then offered application of the principle, couched in several examples drawn from our own church family.

A couple weeks ago a lady stopped by the church building to ask some questions about our new gym floor. After I showed her the floor, we talked for a few minutes. She said, "Fayetteville Christian Church . . . I think my son's baseball coach goes here—Lamar Knight?"

"Yeah, he's one of our faithfuls," I responded.

"He prays with the boys every time they get together. My son just loves him." When Christians live as Christians, the world takes notice.

---

7. David Veerman, "Apply Within," in *The Art and Craft of Biblical Preaching: A Comprehensive Resource for Today's Communicators*, ed. Haddon Robinson and Craig Brian Larson (Grand Rapids: Zondervan, 2005), 285–86.

Not long ago at a local gym I talked with a guy on the next treadmill. In the course of the conversation, I mentioned that I go to this church. The man said, "I think my son's soccer coach goes there. John Panzenhagen?"

"Yeah, he's one of our faithfuls," I answered.

"He's a good example for our kids. Really wears his faith on his sleeve."

When Christians live as Christians, the world takes notice.

Someone else told me, "Oh, Fayetteville Christian Church; I work with Audrey Bates. She talks about your church all the time." Someone else said, "I buy building materials from Larry Coleman. He's so honest and helpful." Somebody else said, "I used to teach with Lin Adams. She really loves the kids in her class. She's one of the best teachers in the county." "Radford Morris, he used to fix my appliances—he's a hardworking, godly man."

When Christians live as Christians, the world takes notice.

I intended that these examples—application by demonstration—would, first, motivate listeners to respond to the text: "I can do that!" I hoped, second, that the examples would spur ideas in listeners concerning ways they might serve as lights in the world—praying with the kids at little league or maintaining honesty in business.

10. Safeguard: Does This Application Give Expectations or Promises Only Where the Text Does?

Recall that in the discussion of application heresies in chapter 4, we discussed "promising the unpromised," which is guaranteeing listeners certain outcomes that biblical teaching does not truly assure, and "moralizing," which is drawing moral exhortations from a text that go beyond a text's intention. These two particular heresies appear so frequently that they merit a final inspection.

The Bible makes numerous promises. It also defines a fair amount of expectations. Nevertheless, preachers often feel compelled to add to the list. Such additions lead listeners astray.

Unbiblical promises result in disappointed Christians. A lady whose marriage had fallen apart told her counselor, "I tried to be submissive. Doesn't the Bible say if a wife submits, she'll have a successful marriage?" She had heard this taught in seminars, but the Bible never makes such a promise.[8] Other preachers have made promises concerning financial success and physical well-being that go beyond what Scripture actually teaches. Before offering a promise in a sermon, the wise preacher will ask himself whether or not the text legitimately offers that particular guarantee—whether or not the promise bears the authority of God. Otherwise, listeners who take the preacher's promise as God's assurance will find disappointment when it does not come to fruition.

Unbiblical expectations result in legalistic Christians. Like the Pharisees of old, many preachers today—with noble intentions—have such a strong desire to protect God's commands that they build a hedge around them with additional, man-made commands. In an effort to protect the Sabbath, for example, Pharisees taught that believers could walk no more than two-thirds of a mile on the holy day. They gave the man-made command the same weight as God's command. Similarly, today's preacher correctly states, "The Bible teaches us to avoid every kind of evil." The same preacher then incorrectly applies, "This means God prohibits you, Christian, from attending any movie produced by evil Hollywood." When preachers give commands

---

8. Haddon Robinson, "The Heresy of Application," in *The Art and Craft of Biblical Preaching*, 307.

What happens in listeners when biblical texts truly impact them?

Will Willimon: If people truly encounter a text, they encounter God in the text. They stand in awe of Him, they recognize their own inadequacy, and they hunger for God's grace.

I remember when I served a church in Suwannee, Georgia, while I was doing graduate work at Emory University. In that church it was custom to have laypeople pray. I loved that—I preached, they heard the Word; now they could do with it what they will. After the sermon one week, this old farmer got up and said, "Lord, we've heard your Word today, and we don't like it. Lord, sometimes you just ask too much of us."

I sat there with tears streaming down my face, thinking, "I've never heard such powerful praying."

He went on, "I guess Lord, if you've got all this in mind for us, you must have some way for us to do it. We can't do anything without your grace." It was just powerful.

Another time somebody criticized me and said, "It bothers me that you chop off so many of your sermons at the end. Sunday was wrong. You needed to do more in the conclusion. I felt it was terribly unfair."

I said, "You read the sermon, didn't you?"

He said, "Yeah."

I said, "That wasn't a fair representation of the sermon, because as soon as I finished preaching, my associate Deborah stood up and said, 'And now we need to pray. Let us pray.' She began something like, 'Lord, when we look over our lives, we get so discouraged. We set out to do good, and some of the worst things we do are in the name of such good. If we sin even when we do good, what hope is there for us? Lord, we know what that hope is . . .'"

Maybe the best preaching we can do is to get people ready to pray.

beyond what God actually outlined, they burden their listeners with pharisaical standards that result in legalistic believers.

Preachers can offer legitimate promises or expectations only where the Bible does. Haddon Robinson's advice from chapter 3 bears repeating: Wise preachers will distinguish between the necessary, probable, possible, improbable, and impossible implications of a text. Preachers should offer necessary implications (promises or expectations) only where the sermon text does.

Chapters 5 and 6 have outlined ten questions that lead the preacher to sermon application with biblical integrity and contemporary relevance. The conclusion of chapter 5 offered an example of how a preacher might answer the first five questions while preparing a sermon from Job 38–42. After reviewing the first five questions and answers below, observe how the process continues with questions 6 through 10.

1. *Biblical teaching*: What did God originally teach through this text?
   - God taught that He is sovereign over all of creation.

2. *Original purpose*: How did God intend this text to affect its original readers?
   - God intended the original readers to see creation as evidence that they could trust Him, even when they didn't understand why life had turned out as it had.

3. *Comparison of audiences*: How do my listeners compare with the original readers?
   - Though few of my listeners have faced tragedy to the extent of Job's, my listeners do sometimes find themselves wondering about the apparent absence of God during times of suffering.

4. *Listener need*: What listener need does this text address?

   • The text addresses the need to sense that something, or Someone, is in control and that life is more than just a series of random, haphazard, sometimes painful events.

5. *Sermon purpose*: What should my listeners think, feel, or do differently after having heard a sermon from this text?

   • After hearing this sermon, listeners should see creation itself as evidence that God is sovereign and trustworthy, even when life doesn't make sense.

6. *Sermon application*: If the sermon accomplished its purpose in specific listeners dealing with specific life situations, how might it look?

   • *Listener 1*: After enduring years of abuse, a sixteen-year-old girl is placed in a home with foster parents who lovingly, compassionately, and patiently care for her. Yet the scars and pain from her past prove difficult to forget. One Sunday afternoon she goes for a walk in the woods—she feels the sunshine, smells the flowers, and hears the birds singing. She thinks, remembers, and clumsily prays. Finally, the hint of a smile appears on the corners of her mouth, and she hums the tune and thinks of the lyrics she learned at the church her foster parents have been taking her to: "Oh Lord my God, when I in awesome wonder, consider all the worlds Thy hands have made . . . How great Thou art!"

   • *Listener 2*: A young husband/father/business owner struggles to balance his various responsibilities. As a result, his neglected marriage has fallen into critical disrepair. One of the husband's Christian friends invites him to a campout with other Christian men. Beneath the night sky, around the campfire, sensing a nearness to God and his brothers that often comes with an encounter with nature, he tells of his mistakes and his struggles. His brothers encircle him, place their hands on his shoulders, and pray for his marriage. Though much work remains, the prayer provides the spark of a renewed commitment to God and to his wife.

- *Listener 3*: A grandmother battling lung cancer isn't sure she has the strength to face one more chemotherapy treatment. At 3 AM she wakes up. After vomiting (yet again), she sits on the back deck and watches the sky. As the stars twinkle and the moon glows, her nausea eases, along with her mind and heart. "The God who placed those stars," she whispers, "and who set the moon aglow holds power beyond any disease. He still reigns." She looks to the heavens, "Dear Daddy, I need you."

7. *Safeguard*: Does this application exalt God?
   - Yes.

8. *Safeguard*: Is this application consistent with the text's teaching and purpose?
   - Yes.

9. *Safeguard*: Will this application motivate and equip listeners to respond to the text?
   - Yes.

10. *Safeguard*: Does this application give promises or expectations only where the text does?
    - Yes.

CHAPTER SEVEN

The Sermon Application Worksheet

The ten questions listed in chapters 5 and 6 provide the raw materials with which we can construct a sermon application worksheet—a tool to assist preachers when they hunch over their desks and wrestle to define effective application for their sermons.

This chapter includes a blank sermon application worksheet, three completed example worksheets, and a few suggestions to help preachers use the worksheet most productively.

Sermon Application Worksheet

Text:

1. *Biblical teaching*: What did God originally teach through this text?

2. *Original purpose*: How did God intend this text to affect its original readers?

3. *Comparison of audiences*: How do my listeners compare with the original readers?

4. *Listener need*: What listener need does this text address?

5. *Sermon purpose*: What should my listeners think, feel, or do differently after having heard a sermon from this text?

6. *Sermon application*: If the sermon accomplished its purpose in specific listeners dealing with specific life situations, how might it look?
   • Listener 1:
   • Listener 2:
   • Listener 3:

7. *Safeguard*: Does this application exalt God? Y/N

8. *Safeguard*: Is this application consistent with the text's teaching and purpose? Y/N

9. *Safeguard*: Will this application motivate and equip listeners to respond to the text? Y/N

10. *Safeguard*: Does this application give expectations or promises only where the text does? Y/N

Example: 2 Timothy 4:1–5

The Roman emperor Nero treated Christians like Hitler treated Jews. Because he ignored Nero's threats and continued preaching boldly, Paul now sat chained in a musty Roman dungeon awaiting probable execution. From this prison, Paul wrote his second letter to Timothy. This letter was more personal than the first, and it bid Timothy to "endure hardship with us" (2 Tim. 2:3).

Paul had helped convert Timothy to Christianity some twenty years before; then a few years later he invited the young man to join him on a missionary journey. Paul recognized great potential in Timothy and sent him to preach and to help lead the church in Ephesus. Though Timothy did not face circumstances as dire as Paul's, Paul knew two things: First, Timothy did indeed face difficulties within his church—teachers of heresy who attempted to undermine Timothy's leadership. Second, Paul saw storm clouds brewing—the persecution Paul experienced in Rome would soon spread throughout the empire. In the coming years, Timothy and other Christian leaders would suffer intense persecution and martyrdom. In light of these circumstances, Paul encouraged Timothy to persevere in his faith and ministry.

In 2 Timothy 4:1–5, Paul showed particular concern that Timothy persevere in preaching. In spite of the circumstances— indeed, *because of* the circumstances—the gospel needed a voice. Through Paul, God had given Timothy that voice—the gift to preach. Paul, therefore, encouraged his son in the faith, "Preach the Word; be prepared in season and out of season" (2 Tim. 4:2).

The following pages exemplify how a preacher might complete a sermon application worksheet in preparation for a sermon based on 2 Timothy 4:1–5.

Sermon Application Worksheet

Text: 2 Timothy 4:1–5

1. *Biblical teaching*: What did God originally teach through this text?
   - God taught Timothy about his responsibility to faithfully preach the Word, which he had been gifted to do, through good times and bad.

2. *Original purpose*: How did God intend this text to affect its original readers?
   - God intended to boost Timothy's resolve to persevere in his preaching ministry in Ephesus, even in the face of challenging circumstances.

3. *Comparison of audiences*: How do my listeners compare with the original readers?
   - Unlike Timothy, my listeners have not necessarily been gifted to preach. Like Timothy, however, my listeners have received specific gifts from God to use in ministry, and they will sometimes find it difficult to use those gifts in the face of struggles.

4. *Listener need*: What listener need does this text address?
   - Listeners need to sense that they can do something significant. And they need to sense this strongly enough that they will persevere in ministry through good times and bad.

5. *Sermon purpose*: What should my listeners think, feel, or do differently after having heard a sermon from this text?

- As a result of hearing this sermon, listeners should resolve to do with all their might what God gifted them to do.

6. *Sermon Application*: If the sermon accomplished its purpose in specific listeners dealing with specific life situations, how might it look?

    - *Listener 1*: A high school senior, a Christian, struggles to discern what career God would have him pursue. His parents and school counselors push him toward careers that would bring large paychecks. After hearing this sermon, he considers how he can use his particular gifts most significantly for the kingdom. For him, teaching school offers the best opportunity to make an impact with his gifts. He resolves, therefore, to diligently pursue teaching.

    - *Listener 2*: A fifty-five-year-old mother, an empty nester, feels a growing conviction to finish well. While she has often served in the church, she recognizes that for years she had maintained a harsh attitude toward the "sinful world." After hearing this sermon, she recognizes that her spiritual gift of mercy offers an opportunity to influence, rather than wag her finger at, the culture. She picks up the phone and offers to volunteer at the local crisis pregnancy center.

    - *Listener 3*: A young, stay-at-home mother lives a particularly hectic life. While she realizes the value of parenting her children, she feels convicted to use her gift of encouragement to help people beyond her own family who face discouraging situations. After hearing this sermon, she resolves to send one card a day to someone needing encouragement. It doesn't sound like much, but over five years she'll have sent almost two thousand cards.

7. *Safeguard*: Does this application exalt God? <u>Y</u>/N

8. *Safeguard*: Is this application consistent with the text's teaching and purpose? <u>Y</u>/N

9. *Safeguard*: Will this application motivate and equip listeners to respond to the text? <u>Y</u>/N

10. *Safeguard*: Does this application give expectations or promises only where the text does? <u>Y</u>/N

Example: Matthew 6:1–18

Jesus entered a world where following God had, for many people, digressed into empty rituals. Though such expressions might impress onlookers, they did little to genuinely connect people with God or God's community. Jesus called believers to embrace an integrated faith that included both the inward and the outward elements of pure discipleship.

This call of Jesus to His followers emerges clearly in the Sermon on the Mount (Matt. 5–7), the first of five major discourses in Matthew's gospel. Throughout his gospel, Matthew pictures Jesus as the Messiah-King, promised by God, coming to establish His reign. Jesus' kingdom, however, held little in common with the earthly kingdoms with which Matthew's readers were familiar. Therefore, the Sermon on the Mount begins by describing the upside-down nature of Jesus' reign—those shunned and scorned by their culture find themselves blessed in Jesus' kingdom (Matt. 5:1–12), and influential in the world (Matt. 5:13–16).

Having provided this foundation concerning the identity of His followers, Jesus confronted the performance-focused

If a preacher were to say, "My applications seem to have no significant impact on my listeners," how would you respond?

Will Willimon: I'd suggest he make certain that he himself isn't standing in the way with superficial applications. The power is in the text, with all its gravity and magnitude.

I remember a woman who heard me preach on forgiveness. She asked me afterward, "You mean to tell me Jesus expects me to forgive my abusive ex-husband, who made my life hell for ten years until I finally left him? I'm supposed to forgive him now?"

I said, "Um, well, forgiveness is a complicated topic, and I, uh, but Jesus said seventy times seven—that's a lot of forgiveness. And He said to forgive your enemies. I don't know that *I'd* say that."

She said, "Just checking. That's what I thought you'd say."

And I can hear Jesus saying to me, "Would you get out of the way? I see a saint here. I see a hero. I'm going to save the world with this woman."

Bob Russell: A man called me one Sunday afternoon and said, "I've been coming to your church for about four months. I persuaded my teenage son to come with us today. After church he was as mad as could be. He was convinced that we had talked to you about his problem, and that was why you preached the sermon you preached today. Would you get on the phone and tell him it's not true?"

Obviously his son had misjudged the situation, but that's the power of the text and the Spirit. "The Word of God is living and active, sharper than any double-edged sword." If, in a sermon, you just say, "I want to talk to you about this problem today," it won't make much difference. But if you unleash the Word of God, there is something about the Bible that is incredibly powerful.

faith common in His day and challenged His listeners to a righteousness not based on empty ritual (Matt. 5:17–20). Though they had rightly avoided outward sins such as murder, adultery, and divorce, their faith remained void of the related matters of the heart—genuine community, pure thoughts, and marital commitment. They had, therefore, committed the very sins they thought they had avoided (Matt. 5:21–48).

In Matthew 6:1–18, Jesus turned His attention toward righteous acts His listeners performed, such as giving, prayer, and fasting. Though the deeds in themselves were honorable, Jesus warned His listeners against performing them with selfish motives, "before men, to be seen by them" (Matt. 6:1). To realign their focus, Jesus taught them to continue giving, praying, and fasting but to do so in a secretive manner so that only God would know. Such realignment would retrain these followers to seek God's applause rather than the applause of other people.

A preacher preparing a sermon on Matthew 6:1–18 might complete a sermon application worksheet like the one below.

Sermon Application Worksheet
Text: Matthew 6:1–18

1. *Biblical teaching*: What did God originally teach through this text?
   - Believers should find motivation for righteous acts—such as giving, praying, and fasting—in their love for God, not in a desire to impress other people.

2. *Original purpose*: How did God intend this text to affect its original readers?
   - God intended listeners to repent of performing righteous acts to please other people and to instead perform these acts to please Him alone.

3. *Comparison of audiences*: How do my listeners compare with the original readers?

   • Though my listeners may not display their religious hypocrisy as blatantly as did Jesus' original audience, my listeners do face temptation to perform righteous acts to be seen by other people.

4. *Listener need*: What listener need does this text address?

   • The text addresses the need to feel approved and affirmed.

5. *Sermon purpose*: What should my listeners think, feel, or do differently after having heard a sermon from this text?

   • As a result of hearing this sermon, listeners should exercise spiritual disciplines motivated solely by their love for God.

6. *Sermon application*: If the sermon accomplished its purpose in specific listeners dealing with specific life situations, how might it look?

   • *Listener 1*: A teenage boy has been in church all his life (and has heard many prayers!). He began volunteering to pray aloud in youth group and at home. After hearing Jesus' teaching, he realized he was most concerned to "sound good" in his prayers—flowery, with impressive words and phrases. In response to this realization, he refrains from praying aloud in public and devotes himself to private prayer (including specific prayer concerning the motives of his heart), until he has rid his heart of this improper motivation.

- *Listener 2*: A sixty-year-old man accumulated a great deal of material wealth. He enjoyed giving it away. After hearing Jesus' words, he realized that what he enjoyed most were the accolades that came when he gave generously. The accolades became his motivation. Having recognized this selfish motivation, he begins giving only in secret. Strangely, he finds even greater enjoyment in giving when he knows that it remains between just him and God.

- *Listener 3*: A middle-aged woman learned about fasting in a Bible study and began fasting once a month. She enjoyed the looks on others' faces when she said no to lunch: "Can't go with you today—I'm fasting." After hearing Jesus' words, she continues fasting but does so in a way that nobody knows and finds more tactful ways to excuse herself from lunch.

7. *Safeguard*: Does this application exalt God? Y/N

8. *Safeguard*: Is this application consistent with the text's teaching and purpose? Y/N

9. *Safeguard*: Will this application motivate and equip listeners to respond to the text? Y/N

10. *Safeguard*: Does this application give expectations or promises only where the text does? Y/N

Example: Daniel 3

In 605 BC, the Babylonians besieged Jerusalem and took the cream of the crop, young, Jewish men, as captives. Shadrach, Meshach, and Abednego found themselves among those ripped from their homes and shipped to the foreign, pagan nation. In

Babylon, the three friends proved trustworthy and reliable. They worked hard. They remained honest. And they progressed into positions with some authority in the Babylonian government.

All continued smoothly for the young men until King Nebuchadnezzar issued a decree that swept Shadrach, Meshach, and Abednego into a dilemma that would leave them either disobedient to their king or disobedient to their God, and facing the consequences. Nebuchadnezzar built an idol nine feet wide and ninety feet high, which probably depicted the god after which the king had been named and of which Nebuchadnezzar considered himself the incarnation—Nabu. Nebuchadnezzar ordered that when the citizens of the kingdom heard music playing, they must bow in worship of the idol. Any who did not bow would face the burning furnace.

Shadrach, Meshach, and Abednego heard the edict of the king. They also knew the commands of their God. Faced with the choice, they chose God, despite Nebuchadnezzar's threatened punishment. Their capacity to choose God in such circumstances hinged on their trust in God's ability ("If we are thrown into the blazing furnace, the God we serve is able to save us from it," Dan. 3:17), and in their commitment to God's sovereignty ("But even if he does not . . . we will not serve your gods or worship the image of gold you have set up," Dan. 3:18). The three friends trusted that God could save them from the furnace. But even if He chose otherwise, they would remain faithful to Him. God graciously chose to save them from the fire.

Sermon Application Worksheet

Text: Daniel 3

1. *Biblical teaching*: What did God originally teach through this text?

- When they recognize God's sovereignty, followers
  of God can obey Him, even in the face of difficult
  consequences.

2. *Original purpose*: How did God intend this text to
   affect its original readers?
   - God intended this text to inspire its original read-
     ers to remain faithful to Him even if such faithful-
     ness resulted in persecution or martyrdom.

3. *Comparison of audiences*: How do my listeners compare with the original readers?
   - Daniel's original readers faced life-threatening
     consequences if they remained faithful to God.
     While my listeners may not face consequences
     quite as frightening (some Christians around the
     world today certainly do, but my listeners prob-
     ably will not), my listeners do face circumstances
     in which obedience to God could bring painful
     results.

4. *Listener need*: What listener need does this text
   address?
   - This text addresses the need to develop the courage
     to remain faithful to God, despite what difficulties
     such faithfulness might bring.

5. *Sermon purpose*: What should my listeners think, feel,
   or do differently after having heard a sermon from this
   text?
   - As a result of hearing this sermon, listeners should
     find the courage to remain faithful to God, despite
     the potential consequences, because they trust in
     God's sovereignty.

6. *Sermon application*: If the sermon accomplished its purpose in specific listeners dealing with specific life situations, how might it look?

   • *Listener 1*: A Christian in his early twenties agreed to serve as the best man in his friend's wedding. He is the only Christian involved. The best man traditionally plans a bachelor party. The other young men pressure him to hire an exotic dancer. He trusts that if he graciously refuses, the sovereign God will protect him from the ridicule and anger and bring some good from the situation. Though the ridicule does come, his insistence on purity opens the door for spiritual conversations with his friends a week later.

   • *Listener 2*: A woman in her late forties meets a friend for coffee before work twice a week. Though they're both Christians, the ladies seldom speak of spiritual matters. Over coffee, the friend excitedly reveals her martial infidelity: "This week I will leave my husband and move in with my soul mate!" The conversation disturbs the woman. Should she confront her friend or simply be supportive? She decides to obey what she believes God has called her to do and leave the results in His hands. "We have to talk," she begins.

   • *Listener 3*: An engineer nearing retirement receives a memo from his boss telling him to scale back on his latest drawings for budgeting purposes. The engineer knows that scaling back will require putting construction workers in physical danger. "Doesn't matter," the boss says. "Just cut those corners; we can't lose this account." To refuse would cost the engineer his job. To give in would cost him his integrity. He keeps his integrity, loses his job, and prays to his sovereign God.

7. *Safeguard*: Does this application exalt God? <u>Y</u>/N

8. *Safeguard*: Is this application consistent with the text's teaching and purpose? <u>Y</u>/N

9. *Safeguard*: Will this application motivate and equip listeners to respond to the text? <u>Y</u>/N

10. *Safeguard*: Does this application give expectations or promises only where the text does? <u>Y</u>/N

What interpretative matters do preachers often overlook when they develop applications?

Haddon Robinson: We often get off track in our applications when we begin by saying, "The Bible answers all our questions." So, we'll start with our questions and then go looking into the Bible for answers.

We'll try to ask Paul, for example, "Can women be ordained?"

Paul says, "Ordained? What are you talking about?"

"You know, Paul, we stand in a circle in the front of the sanctuary on a Sunday evening, then we have cake and punch afterward, and we give the person a fancy certificate to hang on their office wall."

There are many of our questions that the Bible doesn't really address. Our culture is much different, including our church culture. New Testament believers didn't know anything about liturgy, Sunday school, synods, or conventions.

The Bible speaks to many of our questions only indirectly, by way of principle. Therefore it's difficult to figure out how to apply those principles to today's questions.

Suggestions

A few additional thoughts, based on my own experience, might help you use the Sermon Application Worksheet in the most productive manner.

1. Because we cannot accurately complete the worksheet until we have a grasp of the biblical text, we should study and complete our exegetical work on the text before using the worksheet. Thus, we study the text and then complete the worksheet.

2. Because the worksheet provides applications that may help shape the form and flow of the sermon, we should

Vic Pentz: I think many of us need the academic rigor and discipline of constantly asking ourselves, "What does the text really say?" Maybe each week we should all submit our sermons to solid, stern professors who will tell us, "That application has no integrity with the text."

Tom Long: One specific matter I would mention is that I would like to see preachers pay more attention to the literary genre of a text, even in terms of the applications they develop.

Texts speak to us in certain tones. The voice of a lament psalm speaks differently than the voice of apocalyptic literature or of a healing narrative. Sermons, therefore, ought to take different voices; otherwise we will miss the kind of encounter God intends us to have with the text. A lament psalm will want something different from us than a healing story or an apocalyptic text. One may lead to repentance, another to worship, another to cognition. Recognizing the literary genre helps us hear the text's voice and therefore make the application accurately.

complete the worksheet before we flesh out our sermon outlines and manuscripts. Thus, we study the text, complete the worksheet, and then formulate a sermon outline.

3. When I first developed the worksheet, I used it for five or six weeks in a row. This consistent use helped ingrain the principles into my thinking and sermon preparation.

4. After the initial five or six weeks, the application process had become fairly intuitive, such that I no longer needed to use the worksheet every week. I did, however, continue to use it once every month or two to keep the principles fresh in my mind.

5. I have found it helpful to file completed worksheets with my sermon outlines. If I preach a particular sermon a second time, to a different audience, the filed worksheet enables me to easily alter the application to fit the new audience.

CHAPTER EIGHT

Integrating Application into Sermons

The Sermon Application Worksheet discussed in chapter 7 leads the preacher to application with biblical integrity and contemporary relevance. What now? The next step involves inserting this application into a sermon outline or manuscript.

The most effective way to integrate the application varies from sermon to sermon—it's more of an art than a science. Therefore, this chapter will provide no rigid formula. Instead, it will offer five suggestions to help preachers discern how to most effectively integrate application into sermons. Not every sermon will utilize every suggestion; rather, each suggestion represents a tool for the homiletic toolbox that can be pulled out and used whenever the preacher deems best.

"Pre-application" in the Introduction

The preacher might offer "pre-application" early in the sermon. Pre-application involves raising the listener's needs that the text and sermon will help resolve. Pre-application does not resolve the issues—it simply raises them.

"Parishioners come asking two fundamental questions," Keith Wilhite explains, "and the sermon introduction must answer both: (1) What are you talking about? and (2) Why should I listen? . . . The best way to inform people of what we're talking about includes a simultaneous hint of what difference this sermon may make in their lives."[1] Wilhite continues by encouraging the preacher to raise a clear need in the introduction: "Create a hunger for the answer that God will provide to their need."[2]

The fourth question on the Sermon Application Worksheet leads us to consider what particular need the sermon text addresses. This need provides a basis for pre-application.

To return to our second example worksheet, based on Matthew 6:1–18, we discovered that the text addresses the listener's need to feel affirmed and approved. The introduction of a sermon on this text might include pre-application that raises this need.

> My son, who just turned four, has arrived at the "watch me" stage. Countless times each day he demands, "Watch me, watch me!" Sometimes his mother and I will agree to watch, and he'll have to quickly think of something with which to impress us—a summersault, perhaps, or a silly face.
>
> Many of us never grow out of the "watch me" stage. We drive ourselves crazy trying to please other people. If others criticize us—even slightly—the criticism sends us into the doldrums. If others compliment us—even slightly—the compliment sends us into the clouds. Our moods and outlooks, completely at the mercy of how we perceive others' thoughts about us, rise and fall like the tides.
>
> Some call this an "approval addiction"—living in bondage to what other people think of us. It's a difficult way to live. No one wants to live as an approval addict.

---

1. Keith Wilhite, "A Sneak Peak at the Point: Sermon Introductions That Aim at Application," *Preaching*, May–June 1990, 17–18.
2. Ibid., 18.

Such a life barely resembles the life Jesus called us to live. But approval addicts existed even in Jesus' day. During His most famous sermon, The Sermon on the Mount, Jesus addressed the problem and taught a perspective that will help us break our addiction to the approval of other people.

A second way the introduction might include pre-application involves touching on the particular situations imagined in the sixth question of the Sermon Application Worksheet. If a preacher chose this approach for the sermon based on Matthew 6:1–18 (again, the second example from chap. 7), he would describe the specific scenarios he imagined in the worksheet's sixth question, though without resolving them. The sermon's introduction might include pre-application as follows:

> Sometimes believers wake up on an otherwise normal morning and realize that they have been doing all the right things but for all the wrong reasons.
>
> Take, for example, the teenage boy who attended church all his life. During that time, he heard many prayers—most of them filled with flowery words and poetic phrases. As he grew older, he began volunteering to pray before meals at home and in the Sunday evening teen worship service. When people complimented his prayers, his chest swelled. After one such prayer, and one such compliment, it hit him—during that entire prayer he never thought once about God. He thought only of what he might say that would impress everybody else. Prayer is the right thing; but sometimes we wake up and realize that we've been doing the right things for the wrong reasons.
>
> Or maybe you better identify with the sixty-year-old man who's accumulated a great deal of material wealth. He enjoys giving it away to various churches and charities. Yet in a quiet moment, he realizes that what he

Often preachers think of application as something that comes at the end of the sermon. When, in your sermons, do you begin offering application?

Bob Russell: I usually begin in the introduction by previewing the application that will come, trying to build a sense of need in the listeners.

A while back I preached on David blessing his successor, Solomon. Who would be interested in that? In the introduction I tried to create thirst for the message. I said, "Who has to bless their successors? Some of you are near retirement; you are going to have to pass the baton to the next person at work. Some of you are moving to another job, and you've got to pass the baton to your replacement. Those of you who are parents—you pass the baton of faith to your children in the lessons you give every day."

All of the sudden, they know the sermon will deliver applications that will be helpful to their lives.

Vic Pentz: Traditionally, application was saved for the sermon's

enjoys most are the accolades that come when he makes generous gifts. Giving is the right thing; but sometimes we perform right actions with wrong motivations.

Or perhaps you find more in common with the middle-aged woman who learned about fasting in her Bible study. She began fasting one day a month. She enjoys the looks on her coworkers' faces when they invite her to lunch. "Can't go today," she explains; "I'm fasting!" One afternoon, after such a comment, she begins feeling burdened with guilt. Though she refrains from eating food, she does not pray any more that day than any other day. She does not focus to any greater degree on God. Fasting is the right thing, but her motivations were wrong.

conclusion: "In conclusion, today's lesson should impact your life in three ways . . ."

The difficulty with this approach is that listeners will probably not wait until the end of a sermon to hear the application. If a sermon contains no application in its first few minutes, listeners may conclude that the message is irrelevant and mentally check out.

So, I try to bring in application early. I'll raise questions about issues that I know concern them; then I'll say, "We're going to answer these questions as we talk through the text." I can see people lean forward and look me in the eye.

Then, I like to offer applications all the way through the sermon. I find the most effective applications are almost presented like throwaway lines, just asides. As you walk through the text, you come across something and say, "Doesn't that speak to us? Doesn't that address X-Y-Z?" Listeners appreciate this sense of discovery.

Finally, at the end, I hope to say something that drives it home, something arresting and challenging, something for people to take with them throughout the week.

When this realization hits us, how do we correct ourselves? How do we realign our motivations so that we continue doing the right things but we do them for the right reasons?

In His most famous sermon, the Sermon on the Mount, Jesus addressed these situations. He provided a principle that will help us return to performing righteous acts with proper motivations.[3]

---

3. If we choose pre-application that raises specific situations, we must make certain to resolve these situations later in the sermon. Later in this sermon we would describe how it would look if the teenager, the sixty-year-old man, and the middle-aged woman mentioned in the pre-application were to apply Jesus' teaching.

An introduction that includes such pre-application will leave listeners hungry for the answers God provides to their needs.

Explanation and Demonstration

Chapter 1 taught that sermon application explains or demonstrates how biblical teaching should impact listeners' lives. In the sermon, the preacher should consider using both explanation and demonstration.

In some instances, preachers straightforwardly explain how a text might apply to listeners' lives. In these cases, the scenarios imagined when completing the sixth question of the Sermon Application Worksheet provide seed ideas for the applications. The specific situations imagined might not actually appear in the sermon; instead, the preacher explains applications that grow from the imagined situations.

For example, to return once again to the worksheet based on Matthew 6, in the sixth question we imagined this scenario:

> A teenage boy has been in church all his life (and has heard many prayers!). He began volunteering to pray aloud in youth group and at home. After hearing Jesus' teaching, he realized he was most concerned to "sound good" in his prayers—flowery, with impressive words and phrases. In response to this realization, he refrains from praying aloud in public and devotes himself to private prayer (including specific prayer concerning the motives of his heart), until he has rid his heart of this improper motivation.

If we choose to explain the application, rather than demonstrate it, we might include these words in the sermon:

> Maybe you have come to realize that when you pray, you think most of how your words might sound to other people. In fact, you think of impressing other people much more than you think of God. How might you resolve this?

Perhaps you could give up praying publicly for a time, and commit yourself only to private prayer, until your heart has rid itself of the desire to impress others.

The advantage of explaining the applications lies in its clarity. Explanations offer listeners concrete, specific ideas of how they might apply the truth of the text to their lives.

In other instances, preachers demonstrate, by means of real-to-life illustrations, how a biblical teaching impacts contemporary listeners. In these cases we may take the scenarios imagined in the sixth question of the Sermon Application Worksheet and insert them directly into the sermon. To continue the previous example, the preacher might actually paint the picture of the teenage boy who sought to impress others with his prayers and then describe how he solved his particular struggle. Or, if the preacher knows of a true story that demonstrates how the text might apply to listeners, he might use the true story in the sermon.

The advantage of demonstrating the application, rather than just explaining it, lies in its pictures. With real-to-life demonstrations, listeners do not simply hear suggestions of how they might apply the text; they see how the suggestions appear in the nitty-gritty of life. Such pictures empower listeners—"If she can do what this text teaches, I can too"—and lead them to imagine scenarios from their own lives in which the truth of the text might apply.

Sermon application explains or demonstrates how the biblical truth makes a difference in listeners' lives. Both explanation and demonstration bring advantages and will find fruitful use in the preacher's repertoire.

To take this discussion one step farther, we might consider the benefits of using both explanation and demonstration, one right after the other, in the sermon. For example, we might explain, "This text calls us to submit our worldly wealth to the lordship of Christ and then to steward every penny as He, our Master, directs." This explanation leads naturally into a demonstration, "The other day, I had coffee with a lady who took such a step in her faith. Let me tell you about Nancy. . . ."

Bob Russell provides an example in a sermon based on John the Baptist. At this particular point in the sermon, Russell offers application based on John's distinctiveness from his surrounding culture. Note that the explanation leads Russell naturally into a demonstration.

> We need to be distinctive. The world is enamored with things; we need to be distinctive in that we're disentangled from possessions. The world dresses provocatively, sometimes carelessly; we should be distinctive in that we dress modestly. The world's speech is laced with profanity; we should be distinctive in that we don't swear at all. The world indulges its appetite; we're to be distinctive in that we practice self-control.
>
> I found this demonstrated in a restaurant not long ago. I went to eat with some friends when the assistant manager came over to our table. He was obviously drunk. He said, "You're Bob Russell, aren't you?"
>
> "Yes, I am."
>
> "I've been coming to your church for a couple years now. I'm so glad to meet you. You've made a big difference in my life."
>
> When he left, my friends kidded me, "Not big enough of a difference!"
>
> How could he witness for Christ when he was intoxicated? Christians must be distinctive in that we practice self-control.[4]

---

4. Bob Russell, "Application: The Key to Relevant Preaching," workshop presented at the National Preaching Summit, Indianapolis, 2000.

Preachers may choose to explain, demonstrate, or to combine explanation and demonstration to effectively apply biblical truth in their sermons.

Series of Examples

The preacher might consider a series of brief examples that demonstrate how a particular text applies to various situations. When he offers a series of examples, rather than just a single, extended story, this series of brief applications swells into a wave that floods into numerous corners and crevices of listeners' lives.

These brief examples might stand alone, they might precede an extended application, or they might come on the heels of an extended application.

A series of examples that stands alone might proceed as follows:

God calls us to comfort one another with the same comfort we have received from Him. Perhaps you have experienced God's comfort in the aftermath of the pain and wreckage of divorce; you can now comfort others who experience the same pain. Maybe God held you up during a teenage child's rebellious years; you can now comfort other parents as they dread the midnight ring of the telephone. Or, when the doctor used the C-word to describe your disease, you felt stripped of everything except your faith; others facing the same disease would benefit from your story.

Even if you have not experienced a situation identical to those who are hurting, you can take a meal to the mourning family, send a card to the one who lost her job, offer babysitting to the haggard new mother, or sit in the waiting room with a family whose loved one lies on the operating table.

When you look back, you recognize God's comfort in your life. In what situations can you offer that same comfort to others?

In just a few words, this preacher has touched on seven different situations in which God's call to comfort others might apply.

If the preacher wanted to place an extended example either before or after this series of brief examples, a story like this might work:

Not long ago I attended a funeral visitation held to honor a man in our church who had passed away. I stood in line, along with several others from our church family,

How do illustration and application relate to one another?

Haddon Robinson: There is a significant interplay between application and illustration. Instead of just saying, "Here are four things you should do this week," a good application pictures how a truth shows up in life.

I might preach an application like this: "The Bible teaches us not to worship false images. Some images are made of wood, and some images are in your head. The image in your head is more dangerous than the one made of wood. You follow it with a worshipful homage. It consumes you. It's where you find security. You depend on it for prestige. It is the deepest desire of your life."

I haven't said "Here is Donald Trump, and Donald Trump is worshipping Donald Trump," which would be more of an illustration. However the application functions like an illustration because it takes a truth and turns it into a specific picture. Illustrations have to be specific enough so that people say, "Oh, yeah, I see."

to pass along our condolences to the new widow, Nancy. When my turn arrived, I felt unsure what to say. I hugged Nancy and told her that I would continue praying for her and her grieving family. Then I moved on.

At church the next Sunday, Nancy arrived just before the service began and sat in the pew that she had shared with her husband for forty years. She sat alone. Well, she sat alone until Betty came to sit beside her. Betty lost her husband a couple years before. She wept with Nancy, put her arm around her, and patted Nancy's shoulder as only someone who had walked in her shoes could. Through her embrace, Betty extended to Nancy the same comfort she had received from God.

Vic Pentz: There's just something very powerful when your illustrative material not only illustrates but also applies. The story itself—an illustration of how the truth has applied to someone else—becomes for the listeners all they need to find motivation and ideas of how the text might apply in their own lives.

Will Willimon: Some of the best applications just show that it's possible to respond to the text. Stories illustrate options.

Many people are dying for a lack of options. I tell people about Gandhi, when the judge said, "I have to sentence you to six months in jail. I don't want to, but that's the law, and you've broken the law. This is all I can do." Gandhi said, "You could resign. That's an option. Or you could join me in disobeying an unjust law."

We need to keep showing people various possibilities. When a woman's husband dies, she says, "My life is over; there's no reason to live." The preacher can say, "Hey, let me give you some other scenarios of how your life could look from here out."

We're talking about application but in a more dynamic sense.

This extended example would prove helpful for those who have recently faced the death of a loved one. When the preacher couples the extended scenario with the previous series of brief examples, however, the resulting application contains greater power and offers more expansive assistance to more listeners.

In a sermon about forgiving those who have hurt us, a preacher might offer an extended application about loving a neighbor who has spread damaging rumors. The application would constitute at least a paragraph in the sermon manuscript. Then, after this extended application, the preacher may continue by offering a brief series of other scenarios: "These principles also apply to forgiving the guy at work who lied to beat you out of a promotion, the family member who refuses to pay back the money you loaned him, and the former business partner who ruined your career and damaged your reputation."

A series of examples multiplies the number of listeners touched by the application.

Describing Contrasting Situations

Chapter 2 discussed the value of offering possibilities that enhance the work of the Spirit rather than lists that limit the Spirit. When we think of application, we sometimes think only of lists—"Step one, do this. Step two, do that." Such lists hold danger because they might inadvertently imply to listeners that obeying the preacher's list of instructions will solve their every problem, regardless of circumstances, life situations, or the particulars of their struggle. Such lists often ignore the tensions of life and portray faith as easy answers and clichés.

Rather than offering lists, the preacher might describe how the biblical teaching applies in a variety of situations, even situations that stand in direct opposition to one another.

For a father to raise his children in the Lord, for example, will sometimes require words of affirmation and encouragement; at other times it will require discipline. For one person, worshipping another "god" might involve constantly serving others, so that this service becomes her identity and sense of self, to the neglect of her marriage and personal health; for another person the "god" might be herself, so that she serves herself to the neglect of serving others. For many throughout history, presenting their bodies as living sacrifices has involved dying for Christ; for others it has involved living for Christ.

The wise preacher will consider how a biblical teaching applies to a variety of circumstances and will include these various applications in a sermon.

Application Beyond the Sermon

Sometimes the sermon finds its most effective application after the preacher has stepped off the stage. Such application may occur later in a worship service, or it may occur later in the community life of the church.

On some occasions a sermon may lead listeners to apply the biblical teaching during elements of a worship service that follow the sermon. For instance, the preacher may choose such an approach when preaching on 1 Peter 5:7, "Cast all your anxiety on him because he cares for you." Rather than defining application in the sermon itself, the preacher might invite listeners to write their anxieties on a piece of paper after the sermon is completed, and to lay these papers at the foot of a cross that has been erected on the stage.

Application also might come after the sermon in the form of church sacraments. A sermon may naturally lead into a baptism or into the partaking of the Lord's Supper. Will Willimon explains concerning his own experience,

How does sermon application relate to a preacher's pastoral relationship with a congregation?

Will Willimon: Sermons don't just begin and end in that thirty-minute time slot on Sunday mornings. They continue throughout the life of a healthy congregation. Some of my best preaching occurred at, say, a Wednesday evening church supper, when a church member mentioned in conversation something about the sermon.

We should also realize that if we are not in a pastoral relationship with a person, even the applications within a sermon may not connect. I remember one Sunday, when I was in local ministry in Myrtle Beach, I preached on Jesus' teaching about divorce. After the sermon I stood at the door and shook hands with people as they went out. A group of six tourists stood in a line to tell me that it was the most insensitive, cruel sermon they'd ever heard. "Do you not have any divorced people in this congregation?"

I said, "Yeah, and they loved it."

But then I realized that these tourists didn't know me as a pastor. The people in the church know me. They know that

We have communion once or twice a month. And it's peculiar—I am free to preach stronger, more prophetic sermons then than at any other time of the year. I'm free to say, "Here's a text on judgment. Let me slug you in the stomach with judgment." Listeners respond, "Oh my, I'm a failure, what can I do?" I say, "Here, open your hands, the body of Christ. You're hungry. You're empty. Feed. There'll be a time for new year's resolutions and all, but for now just receive the body and blood. Feed on Him."

There are so many Scripture texts that we shouldn't dare go out and preach unless we come to the Lord's

when the first plate is thrown in a marital argument, I hear it. I'm there the next morning, "Can we talk?" I go with them to court if it comes to that. I'm with them all the way through it. I've earned the right to preach what I preached.

Tom Long: I remember one Sunday morning when I ministered in a local parish. Two hours before church one of our elders died while jogging. I ran to the hospital, comforted the widow, and made arrangements to talk to her later that afternoon. Then I went to church. I began the service by telling the congregation, "Sam is dead." At that point I didn't throw my sermon away, but I changed it on my feet. This was a small congregation, and everybody loved Sam. We needed to grieve.

A twenty-something woman who'd been visiting for a couple weeks told me later, "I didn't get a thing out of that sermon."

We could panic or have self-doubt about such a comment.

Instead, I tried to sensitively explain, "That's probably what you should've gotten out of it—nothing. We were attempting as a congregation to deal with grief, and you aren't a part of the congregation yet." Without the presence of a pastoral relationship, a sermon loses much of its power to connect.

Table. The texts have no business out there alone. If you don't come to the bread and cup, you have nowhere to take loneliness, your need.[5]

When we intend listeners to apply the sermon in later elements of a worship service, we might explain this intention to make certain that the listeners cross the bridge with us: "God intends this text to send us to our knees in prayer. Would you bow your heads and pray to the Father?" Or, "This passage

---

5. From an interview conducted with Will Willimon at Duke University in Durham, North Carolina.

calls to mind the grace offered through the cross of Jesus Christ. It would be most appropriate for us now to remember the cross in the manner Jesus established—through the cup and bread."

In addition to sermons finding application later in a worship service, they also may find application later in the life of the church. Preaching occurs as a part of the preacher's ministry. Though occasionally a guest preacher passes through without having developed significant relationships with the listeners, on most occasions the person preaching the sermon enjoys a pastoral relationship with the listeners. Even in large congregations, where the preacher may not know every individual personally, the preacher usually will have significant relationships with at least some in the community, enough so that he carries a certain ethos into the pulpit: "He lives among us. He's one of us. He knows us. He loves us."

The preacher's involvement with the community certainly will impact the applications he develops in the sermon; however, it also impacts applications that may come after the sermon through conversations in the hallway, over lunch, or through e-mails swapped throughout the week. When a member of a congregation begins a conversation with, "I've been thinking about what you said Sunday," the door has flown open for application that plays out through the pastoral relationship.

Not long ago, I preached a sermon about believers encouraging one another. A few days later, I ran across an older church member. "You talked last Sunday about encouragement," he began. "The whole time I kept looking over at the group of teenagers in our church. I kept feeling convicted that God wants me to be an encourager to the next generation. Some of them have things pretty tough, and most of us old codgers just sneer at them. I want to change this. I want to encourage them. But how can I do that?" His question sparked a ten-minute conversation in which we shared several ideas—specific applications sparked by the previous Sunday's sermon—about how he might encourage the teens in the church.

Application often occurs beyond the confines of the formal sermon.

Once we have used the Sermon Application Worksheet to develop applications, we must implement these applications into our sermon outlines and manuscripts. While this is more of an art than a science, the suggestions provided in this chapter should help.

Concluding Thoughts

I began this journey frightened by sermon application. Eight chapters later I'm a little less frightened, a little less intimidated, and a great deal more convicted concerning the need for effective sermon application.

In this book's introduction, we established a goal to construct a tool that would help us develop application with biblical integrity and contemporary relevance. Toward that end we created the Sermon Application Worksheet. Take it. Use it. Revise it. Improve it. Share it.

As you hunker down in your study week after week and stand before your congregation Sunday after Sunday, know that I pray for you. I pray that your preaching will exalt Christ. I pray that His Spirit will empower you and your listeners. I pray that the proclamation of His Word will change lives, beginning with yours and mine.

Sample Sermon

The sermon below incorporates the principles discussed in this book, showing how use of the Sermon Application Worksheet influences an actual sermon.

This appendix will present (1) a description of the occasion on which I preached the sermon, (2) a brief discussion of the text from which the sermon grows, (3) a sermon application worksheet based on the text, (4) the sermon itself with running commentary in shaded boxes that discusses the thoughts and decisions that lay behind various elements of the sermon, and (5) an example of how the applications might vary for the same sermon preached to a different audience.

Occasion

I had the opportunity to preach for a homecoming service at the church in which my wife committed her life to Christ as a high schooler—First Christian Church in Carmi, Illinois. I had met a few church members briefly, but I did not know them well. However, I assumed that those in attendance on the Sunday I preached faced the difficulties and tensions that most American Christians face. Though our lives with Christ should bring great adventure, we often allow them to fall into mundane and comfortable exercises of religion. Deep down, we desire a more sacrificial faith. We sense the Spirit pulling us to venture beyond the shallow end and into the deeper currents of discipleship. We usually ignore this conviction, however, and continue muddling about in our routine existence.

To learn more about this specific congregation, I researched the church's history on the church's web site. I discovered that the congregation enjoyed a rich history that stretched back to 1851, when a few believers began meeting in a living room. Soon a preacher from a neighboring town began traveling each Sunday in his horse-drawn buggy to minister with the fledgling congregation. As the church grew, they moved from the living room to the local courthouse, then they built their own building. Today the congregation continues to thrive in its small Midwest farm town, averaging around three hundred and fifty attendees every weekend.

Additionally, I knew the church recently had faced some painful struggles that led to the resignation of a staff member. The church endured these difficulties, however, and continues ministering and making a significant impact on their community.

Background of Text

In the gospel that bears his name, Matthew paints a portrait of Jesus as the Messiah-King, foretold by the prophets, who came to launch His kingdom through His life, teaching, death, and resurrection. Matthew hoped to lead his primarily, though not exclusively, Jewish readers to a discipleship deeper than the superficial and to a commitment beyond the comfortable.

Matthew emphasized that subjects of Jesus' kingdom approach life and faith in a manner opposite of the self-important, egocentric lifestyles the world so readily applauds. Jesus begins the Sermon on the Mount, His manifesto for kingdom subjects, with the words, "Blessed are the poor in spirit, for theirs is the kingdom of heaven" (Matt. 5:3). Ultimately, discipleship for Jesus' followers requires a cross—a complete sacrifice of one's self for the sake of the kingdom. Jesus taught, "Anyone who does not take his cross and follow me is not worthy of me" (Matt. 10:38). And, "If anyone would come after me, he must deny himself and take up his cross and follow me. For whoever wants to save his life will lose it, but whoever loses his life for me will find it" (Matt. 16:24–25).

The particular text of this sermon, Matthew 26:36–46, portrays Jesus praying in Gethsemane, agonizing over the cross He would face in just a few hours. The kingdom characterized by followers who take up their crosses will be inaugurated by the King who takes up His. This truth does not imply that our sacrifice compares to Jesus' sacrifice; He bore the sins and guilt of the world—a gesture far more painful and expansive than we could possibly emulate. It does imply, however, that the complete self-sacrifice of both the King and His subjects lies at the heart of Christianity.

When we consider the application for a sermon on this passage, we recognize first and foremost that the passage sends us to our knees in worship and gratitude, mindful of the agony Jesus accepted on our behalf and for our salvation. When we place this text in the larger context of Matthew's gospel, we also recognize that Jesus' agony in Gethsemane provides an example of the submission that He demands of His followers. Every kingdom subject who dares to venture into the deeper currents of discipleship will pray, "Not as I will, but as you will" (Matt. 26:39).

Sermon Application Worksheet

Text: Matthew 26:36–46

1. *Biblical teaching*: What did God originally teach through this text?
   - The kingdom requires complete submission—something exemplified in a radical manner by the King Himself.

2. *Original purpose*: How did God intend this text to affect its original readers?
   - God intended the original readers to recognize the sacrificial nature of Christ's kingship, leading them to follow His example of sacrifice.

3. *Comparison of audiences*: How do my listeners compare with the original readers?
   - Like Matthew's readers, my listeners need to be reminded consistently of the deep implications of following Jesus.

4. *Listener need*: What listener need does this text address?
   - Listeners need to regain the sense of adventure in following Christ radically and sacrificially.

5. *Sermon purpose*: What should my listeners think, feel, or do differently after having heard a sermon from this text?
   - As a result of this sermon, listeners should, in worshipful response to Jesus' submission to the cross, submit themselves to following Him sacrificially.

6. *Sermon application*: If the sermon accomplished its
   purpose in specific listeners dealing with specific life
   situations, how might it look?

   - *Listener 1*: A man in his thirties operates his own
     business and has met with moderate financial suc-
     cess. Over a period of several months, however, he
     began to feel God convicting him toward foreign
     mission work. When a missionary couple spoke
     at his church, their stories, pictures, and passion
     only further ignited the conviction in his heart.
     One night that next week, he couldn't sleep; so he
     took a walk outside. In his heart he argued with
     himself about the possible, major life change. His
     mind filled with questions to which he had no
     answers. In addition to these questions, however,
     he couldn't shake a single, transformative image
     from his mind—the cross. Finally, beneath the light
     of the moon, he fell to his knees and prayed, "Not
     as I will, but as you will."

   - *Listener 2*: A woman in her late forties has served
     faithfully in the church as long as she can remem-
     ber. She participates in workdays to help spruce
     up church grounds and teaches a children's Sunday
     school class every week. However, she has a grow-
     ing conviction about serving those who may never
     step into a church building. A couple times a month
     she travels for business to a neighboring, large city.
     Lately the plight of the homeless in that city has
     touched her heart. The thought of reaching out to
     them frightens her, but she can't rid her heart of
     the nagging conviction. One afternoon she pulls
     her car to the side of the road, caresses the cross
     on her bracelet, and prays, "Father, I don't know

what I'm getting myself into. But if this is what you want me to do, I give myself to serve as a tool in your hands."

- *Listener 3*: An older man has attended the same church since he was a toddler. He knows many people; many people know him. He gets along with most people most of the time. As sometimes happens in churches, however, at a meeting a few months ago he had a difference of opinion with another longtime member. In their younger days they had fished together, but church business has left them at odds more than once over the last twenty years. God has been convicting him, however, to humble himself, apologize, and reconcile with his old friend. One Sunday, while celebrating the Lord's Supper, he looks across the aisle at his former fishing buddy, and prays, "Lord, not my will, but yours be done."

7. *Safeguard*: Does this application exalt God? Y/N

8. *Safeguard*: Is this application consistent with the text's teaching and purpose? Y/N

9. *Safeguard*: Will this application motivate and equip listeners to respond to the text? Y/N

10. *Safeguard*: Does this application give expectations or promises only where the text does? Y/N

Sample Sermon: "How Far?"

Matthew 26:36–46

I feel honored to worship and study with you today. Thank you for the privilege of sharing in your homecoming celebration.

For many years I have thought highly of First Christian Church. Through your ministry and outreach, my wife committed herself to following Christ when she was in high school. Thank you for the blessing, guidance, and encouragement you gave her at a critical point in her life. What I hope is the second happiest day of her life also occurred right here in this sanctuary; she and I were married here in 1994.

You have ministered admirably in this community since 1851, when a small band of believers began meeting in the home of Mary Robinson. Your first preacher, Alfred Flower, drove his horse and buggy to Carmi from Albion. Soon thereafter you moved into the White County Courthouse, then into a wood-frame building, then into a block building, and eventually you moved here.

You have ministered for well over one hundred and fifty years—touching countless lives, baptizing new believers, celebrating weddings, conducting funerals, comforting the hurting, offering guidance to the aimless, teaching God's truths. For over one and a half centuries you have worshipped and served Jesus Christ.

Some of those years proved more difficult than others. You faced some struggles that would have caused many churches to crumble. But you endured. You persevered. You stayed true to your calling to worship and serve God. You stayed true to the preaching of the gospel. And today, you continue serving and preaching and worshipping and loving. You are a church—Christ's church. I admire you.

I chose to begin the sermon in this manner for two reasons. First, in this "sermon before the sermon," I hoped that informing listeners of my appreciation and admiration of their rich history would enable me to develop a rapport with them, even though we did not know one another very well. Second, because the sermon would later offer fairly direct challenges, these opening words would help to set those challenges in a positive rather than a negative context.

Because I admire you, I hope today to stretch you a little further. A good coach pushes the best athletes the most because he sees their potential. This morning I hope to do the same with you. You minister and serve as an admirable, exemplary church. Your history of faithfulness hints toward your great potential for future ministry.

With this history and potential in mind, I hope today to stretch you with a simple question: How far will you follow God? More specifically, will you follow God to the other side of the world? To the other side of the tracks? To the other side of the aisle? How far—when it comes down to it, when all the chips are down, when the rubber meets the road—how far will you follow God?

I can imagine a member of First Christian Church. The business you started fifteen years ago has met with success. You set goals for your career and for your checking account—for the most part, you have met these goals. You may not drive a brand-new car every year, but you do every couple years. You may not live in a mansion, but your house offers more than adequate comfort.

Over the last few months, however, God has tugged on your heart. Maybe you encountered a missionary at a camp or a conference. Perhaps a magazine article that told of the global need for Christ caught your attention and your conscience. Your heart began racing on that evening when you stood in a prayer circle in your small group and you heard someone pray that God would raise up more workers for the harvest.

You have arrived at the frightening conclusion that more important than living luxuriously is living significantly. Outside your window exists a world—an entire globe full of people— that needs to hear about Christ and His cross.

Numerous question marks pop up. Where should I go? What's it take to be a missionary? How do I raise support? What if I don't fit into the culture? Will I have to learn a new language? What about my family? My career? Many question marks . . . but one exclamation point: God is calling you!

How far will you follow God? Will you follow Him to the other side of the world? To the other side of the tracks? To the other side of the aisle? How far will you follow God?

> *This is an example of pre-application, drawn straight from question six of the Sermon Application Worksheet. The sermon will offer all three scenarios imagined in that question on the worksheet; then the sermon's conclusion will picture the three people submitting themselves to Christ's conviction on their hearts. Also, the questions (Will you follow Him to the other side of the world? The tracks? The aisle?) hint to the listener what direction the sermon will go.*

I cannot help but think of a particular Scripture text—that striking scene from Matthew 26 that describes Jesus wrestling with the task that lay before Him.

Moments earlier Jesus had gathered with His disciples in an upper room in Jerusalem. He washed their feet, and established the Lord's Supper. He laughed with them, spoke earnestly with them, prayed with them, and sang with them.

As night fell, they left the Upper Room and hiked to the Mount of Olives, a hillside lush with olive orchards just outside of Jerusalem. David wept on this hillside while his son Absalom led a rebellion below. Ezekiel and Zechariah envisioned the glory and power of God resting on the mount. Just days before Jesus went there with His disciples, Jesus had ridden by the Mount of Olives during His triumphal entry. The hillside probably provided the branches people waved as Jesus entered the city on a donkey.

But the scene on this night, the night before Jesus' crucifixion, brought passions and emotions of a drastically different flavor.

On the lower portion of the Mount of Olives rested a garden called Gethsemane (which means "olive press"), where workers brought olives from the orchards and dumped them into a press that extracted their oil.

Matthew explains that after they left the Upper Room, "Jesus went with his disciples to a place called Gethsemane, and he said to them, 'Sit here while I go over there and pray.' He took Peter and the two sons of Zebedee along with him, and he began to be sorrowful and troubled. Then he said to them, 'My soul is overwhelmed with sorrow to the point of death. Stay here and keep watch with me'" (Matt. 26:36–38).

With eleven disciples following Him, Jesus arrived at the Mount of Olives. The men trudged up the slope until they arrived at the gates of Gethsemane. Jesus instructed eight of the disciples to remain there.

Jesus then took three a little farther—Peter, James, and John. Jesus had taken these three a little farther on at least two prior occasions. Of Jesus' twelve disciples, only these three witnessed Him raising Jairus's daughter from the dead. Later, only these three witnessed the Transfiguration, catching a glimpse of Jesus' deity—He is the Son of God. On this night, in Gethsemane, they would catch a glimpse of Jesus' humanity—He is the Son of Man.

Peter, James, and John all had previously told Jesus they would remain committed to Jesus even unto death. Jesus needed their support, encouragement, and presence now more than ever. Jesus faced a decision—among the olive presses, in the darkness. Will He complete the task that lay before Him? Accept the cup of the Father's wrath? Give His life on the cross? Or will He back out? He could have, you know—backed out, packed up, given in.

The weight of the world pressed on Jesus' shoulders that night.

All of us face life-changing choices at one time or another. Oh, your decision may not seem as monumental as Jesus' dilemma in Gethsemane. When God calls you to follow Him further than you have ever followed Him before, however, you face a decision that at least reflects Jesus' dilemma. As Jesus agonized over His impending crucifixion, you wrestle with the question: how far will you follow God?

The sermon periodically shifts from the ancient scene of Gethsemane to the contemporary context of the listeners in the pews. At this point in the sermon, listeners may not yet see how the two connect. Later, however, the sermon will attempt to make the connection abundantly clear.

The paragraphs below paint the picture drawn from the second scenario imagined in the sixth question of the Sermon Application Worksheet, and then return to the series of questions that tie the sermon and its applications together.

I can imagine a member of First Christian Church. You have served faithfully in the church for some time now. You show up for workdays; you take your turn teaching the Sunday school class. You pitch in and help with the dishes after potluck dinners.

Yet, in the midst of all this church activity, you have a nagging sense that you have missed something. You sometimes travel on business—often to Evansville, occasionally to St. Louis or Indianapolis. The last time you traveled, you found yourself in the socially depressed side of town, on the other side of the tracks. You watched a woman and her small child as they sat on cardboard beneath a bridge and ate from a McDonald's bag that looked as though it had been retrieved from a dumpster. They have never been to Sunday school at your church, and they never stop by for potluck dinners. But they need someone to care, someone to feed them, someone to teach them, someone to love them.

You pull your car to the side of the road. Your eyes begin to swell. You fidget with the cross on your bracelet. How far will you follow God? Will you follow Him to the other side of the world? To the other side of the tracks? To the other side of the aisle?

Matthew describes Jesus as "sorrowful and troubled" in Gethsemane (Matt. 26:37). These English words barely do justice to the original language. The Greek terms Matthew originally used describe deep, painful, knock-you-to-your-knees anguish. The next verse better describes His pain. There, Jesus confessed, "My soul is overwhelmed with sorrow to the point of death" (Matt. 26:38).

Why such anguish? Jesus knew that later in the evening He would stand trial and the next day He would face a scourging that would leave Him gasping for life. Then, soldiers would brutally nail Jesus' hands and feet to a splintery cross.

I tend to believe, however, that something troubled Jesus even more deeply than the prospect of physical pain. Yes, the scourging and crucifixion would send bolts of agony throughout His body—we must not minimize the physical suffering Jesus faced. But something more complex and infinitely more excruciating would occur on that cross.

While on the cross, Jesus would have thrust onto His shoulders the guilt incurred by the sins of all of mankind of all generations. The guilt of sin brings enormous spiritual pain. Perhaps you have felt that sting in your heart that comes with sin, that knife in your conscience. To imagine what Jesus experienced, multiply the pain of your guilt by the billions of people who have walked the earth and the billions upon billions of sins we have committed.

Furthermore, consider that sin separates man and God. Because Jesus lived without sinning, He had never experienced that separation. But as He prayed in Gethsemane, Jesus knew that in just a few hours, as He took upon His shoulders the sins of the world, that sin would drive a vile wedge between Him and the Father. "My God, my God," He would cry out, "why have you forsaken me?" (Matt. 27:46).

In Gethsemane, anticipating what lay ahead, Jesus fell face-down and prayed in such agony that, as another gospel writer describes it, "his sweat was like drops of blood falling to the ground" (Luke 22:44).

Note the content of His prayer:

> Going a little farther, he fell with his face to the ground and prayed, "My Father, if it is possible, may this cup be taken from me. Yet not as I will, but as you will."
>
> Then he returned to his disciples and found them sleeping. "Could you men not keep watch with me for one hour?" he asked Peter. "Watch and pray so that you will not fall into temptation. The spirit is willing, but the body is weak."
>
> He went away a second time and prayed, "My Father,

if it is not possible for this cup to be taken away unless I drink it, may your will be done."

When he came back, he again found them sleeping, because their eyes were heavy. So he left them and went away once more and prayed the third time, saying the same thing.

Then he returned to the disciples and said to them, "Are you still sleeping and resting? Look, the hour is near, and the Son of Man is betrayed into the hands of sinners. Rise, let us go! Here comes my betrayer!" (Matt. 26:39–46).

"My Father," Jesus prayed, "if it is possible, may this cup be taken from me. Yet not as I will, but as you will." The cup represents the wrath of physical and spiritual anguish that God would pour onto Jesus during the crucifixion. Jesus offered this prayer to the Father three times, each time His appeal hinging on its final statement, that ultimate expression of submission: "Not as I will, but as you will."

In the midst of the three prayers, Jesus returned twice to find Peter, James, and John sleeping. Though they said they would die for Jesus, on this night they could not even stay awake for Him.

With Jesus' agonizing cries hanging in the air above the olive groves, Judas marched up the hill, soldiers in tow. Jesus stood and strode toward Judas. Jesus didn't run away. He didn't stumble. He didn't hesitate. He faced the cross head-on.

He went that far for us. How far will we follow Him?

Paul spent the first eleven chapters of his monumental letter to the Romans discussing the cross and its implications. When he arrived at chapter 12, Paul made clear how believers should respond to the mercy we have received through the cross: "I urge you, brothers, in view of God's mercy, to offer your bodies as living sacrifices, holy and pleasing to God—this is your spiritual act of worship" (Rom. 12:1). The message is clear: Christ's complete sacrifice demands our complete sacrifice.

Up to this point, listeners probably have caught on that Jesus serves as our example of submission. With these last few paragraphs, hopefully, they begin to sense that Jesus also serves as our motivation. We give ourselves as an expression of worship, in gratitude for the cross and the grace Jesus offers us through the cross.

My primary struggle with this sermon involved maintaining a Christological focus, rather than an anthropological focus. The text teaches about Jesus. I did not want to take the spotlight away from Him.

When we encounter the truth of the cross, however, the encounter carries enormous implications for our behavior. Truth brings implications; imbedded within indicatives are imperatives (recall our discussion from chap. 3). In this case, we sacrifice ourselves (imperative) like and because He sacrificed Himself (indicative). Though I did not want to lose the Christological focus, the Romans 12 passage warranted, I felt, the anthropological applications.

I can imagine a member of First Christian Church. You have attended church here since you were a toddler. You know many people; many people know you. You get along with most people most of the time. As sometimes happens in churches, however, at a meeting a few months ago you had a difference of opinion with another longtime member—a friend with whom you used to fish in your younger days. Differing opinions led to raised voices, hurt feelings, and a damaged friendship. Church business has left you at odds with one another more than once over the last twenty years. Since this last meeting you have exchanged a couple awkward hellos in the hallway, but the relationship remains strained.

Every time you open your Bible, it seems to fall to one of those passages—"Do not let the sun go down while you are still angry" (Eph. 4:26); "Go and be reconciled to your brother" (Matt. 5:24); and "Whoever loves God must also love his brother" (1 John 4:21). Just this morning when you held the bread and the juice in your hands, contemplating the implications of the cross on your life with God and God's people, you looked up and saw, just across the aisle from you, your former friend.

How far will you follow God? Will you follow Him to the other side of the world? To the other side of the tracks? To the other side of the aisle?

I hoped this third scenario, at first glance less weighty than the previous two, would help listeners see that the truth of Jesus' death carries implications not only for those who would leave their careers for the foreign mission field or for those who would begin ministering to the homeless. The idea of submitting ourselves to God carries implications related even to those "smaller" matters, such as our relationships within the church community.

The applications have progressed from the apparent "large" to the apparent "small"—following God to the other side of the world, to the other side of the tracks, and then to the other side of the aisle—to illustrate that our submission to God carries implications for all aspects of our lives.

The paragraphs below tie the sermon together with the thesis statement (in bold print), and then describe what sacrifice looked like for a series of biblical characters and what it might look like in the three scenarios imagined in the applications, thus bringing the applications full circle.

I can answer the question for you, you know. I can define precisely how far you will follow God. The answer comes straight from our text. How far will you follow God? *You will follow God as far as you will pray, "Not as I will, but as you will."* You will follow God to the extent that you will deny yourself and take up your cross, to the extent that you will crucify yourself with Him, to the extent that you will call Him "Lord" and mean it. You will follow God as far as you will pray, "Not as I will, but as you will."

What will this submission look like? It will look like Abraham and his caravan fading into the distant horizon, a day's journey from Ur, following God only God knows where. It will look like young David caressing five smooth stones between his fingers, James and John tossing their nets into a heap beneath the bow of their father's boat and scurrying after the Nazarene, Timothy kissing his mother on the cheek in Lystra, throwing his knapsack across his shoulder and venturing after the apostle Paul.

Submission will look like a member of First Christian Church stepping off an airplane onto foreign soil, heart fluttering but eyes fixed intently on the harvest; a member of First Christian Church rising before dawn three mornings a week to switch on the gas stove to scramble a few dozen eggs to serve a few dozen people downtown who have nowhere else to go but who have just begun to gain a glimpse of the grace of Jesus Christ; a member of First Christian Church, after the final note of this morning's closing song, stepping across the aisle and embracing his old fishing buddy. "I'm so sorry," he begins.

Submission will look like you and me going back to our houses or apartments, going into our rooms, falling to our knees, resting our elbows on the bed and our head in our hands, and praying, "Not as I will, but as you will."

I intended for these final images, first, to remind listeners that when they submit to God they stand in the legacy of believers who have done the same for centuries, including many biblical characters. Second, I hoped these images would help listeners see clearly what submission to Christ might look like for them. These applications come in the form of demonstration rather than explanation.

Application Altered for a Different Audience

I also preached this Matthew 26 sermon in a chapel service at the Bible college where I teach. I left much of the sermon unchanged but used three applications that, though they hold much similarity with the applications above, better fit a college audience.

I include these variations from the Matthew 26 sermon to demonstrate how the Sermon Application Worksheet can help preachers modify a sermon's applications in relation to the audience. The three scenarios below were sprinkled throughout the sermon, then wrapped up at the end, similar to the applications in the sermon above.

How far will you follow God? Will you follow God to the other side of the world? To the other side of the tracks? To the other side of the hallway?

I can imagine a Johnson Bible College student. When you first came to Johnson, you planned to stay only one year—primarily to appease your parents and your minister back home. Then, you planned to attend pharmacy school. Oh, ministry is fine, for people who like that kind of thing. But not you. You wanted the Lexus, the vacation home, the Rolex.

But over the last few months, God has tugged on

your heart. Maybe you first felt the tug during Missions Emphasis Week last semester. Everyone joined hands in a big circle and prayed that God would raise up more workers for the harvest. Or, maybe you felt the tug when you overheard other students in the cafeteria talk about their summer internships on foreign fields.

Regardless of when you first felt the tug, you have arrived at the frightening conclusion that more important than living luxuriously is living significantly. Outside your window exists a world—an entire globe full of people—that needs to hear about Christ and His cross.

Numerous question marks pop up. Where should I go? What's it take to be a missionary? How do I raise support? What if I don't fit into the culture? What about my family? Many question marks . . . but one exclamation point: God is calling you!

I can imagine a Johnson Bible College student. You came to Johnson with visions of serving as a youth minister in a megachurch. You have already made notes about what you'll preach when you receive invitations to speak at large youth conferences. You've considered how you'll respond when *Christianity Today* interviews you concerning ministry to today's teens.

This semester, however, you have begun to sense a change in your heart and your focus. To meet a class requirement, you volunteered at a homeless ministry downtown, on the other side of the tracks. Your buddy chose this particular ministry, or perhaps the gal you hoped to get a date with, so you went. The ministry changed you—your perspective of life, of success. The men, women, and children you encountered there never attend the major youth conferences. They don't read *Christianity Today*. Yet, they need someone to care, someone to teach them, someone to love them—and not just for an hour a week for class credit.

I can imagine a Johnson Bible College student, nearing the end of your college career. Your studies have gone well. You've learned a great deal about the Bible and various academic disciplines. You've developed skills you'll need for ministry and leadership. You have grown in your love for God and for other people.

Over the last few weeks, however, God has convicted your heart. Your friend lives across the hallway from you in the dorm. The two of you have grown fairly close during your time at school. You know, however, that your friend has been pushing the limits sexually with her boyfriend. You believe that God, in His Word, calls you to sit down with your friend and have a difficult conversation. Yet, every time you reach toward the doorknob to make that increasingly longer walk across the hallway, you find an excuse.

How far will you follow God? Will you follow God to the other side of the world? To the other side of the tracks? To the other side of the hallway?

Bibliography

Adams, Jay E. *Truth Applied: Application in Preaching*. Grand Rapids: Zondervan, 1990.

Aycock, Don M., ed. *Heralds to a New Age: Preaching for the Twenty-first Century*. Elgin, IL: Brethren Press, 1985.

Barth, Karl. *Homiletics*. Louisville: Westminster/John Knox Press, 1991.

Bonhoeffer, Dietrich. *Worldly Preaching: Lectures on Homiletics*. Revised. New York: Crossroad, 1991.

Brooks, Phillips. *The Joy of Preaching*. Grand Rapids: Kregel, 1989.

Buerlein, Homer K. *How to Preach More Powerful Sermons*. Philadelphia: Westminster Press, 1986.

Callahan, Kennon L. *Preaching Grace: Possibilities for Growing Your Preaching and Touching People's Lives*. San Francisco: Jossey-Bass, 1999.

Chapell, Bryan. "Application Without Moralism: How to Show the Relevance of the Text." *PreachingToday.com*, May–June 2002. http://www.preachingtoday.com/UserReference=7A9C2DE 641A3F9B63F9EC327&_function=journal&_op=article& res=200203.25 (accessed October 28, 2003).

———. *Christ-Centered Preaching: Redeeming the Expository Sermon*. Grand Rapids: Baker, 1994.

Chapell, Bryan, Haddon Robinson, and Joe Stowell. "Apply

Within." *PreachingToday.com*, January, 2000. http:www
.preachingtoday.com/index.taf?_userreference= 7A9C2DE641
A3F9B63F9EC327&_function=journal&_op=article&res
=200006.1 (accessed October 28, 2003).

Claypool, John. *The Preaching Event*. San Francisco: Harper and
Row, 1989.

Craddock, Fred B. *One Without Authority*. Revised. St. Louis:
Chalice Press, 2001.

———. *Overhearing the Gospel*. Revised. St. Louis: Chalice Press,
2002.

———. *Preaching*. Nashville: Abingdon Press, 1985.

Eslinger, Richard L. *The Web of Preaching: New Options in
Homiletic Method*. Nashville: Abingdon Press, 2002.

Estes, Daniel J. "Audience Analysis and Validity in Application."
Bibliotheca Sacra 150, no. 598 (April–June 1993): 219–29.

Farris, Stephen. *Preaching That Matters: The Bible and Our
Lives*. Louisville: Westminster John Knox Press, 1998.

Fee, Gordon. *Gospel and Spirit: Issues in New Testament Hermeneutics*. Peabody, MA: Hendrickson, 1991.

Fee, Gordon, and Douglas Stuart. *How to Read the Bible for All
Its Worth: A Guide to Understanding the Bible*. Grand Rapids: Zondervan, 1982.

Freeman, Harold. "Making the Sermon Matter: The Use of Application in the Sermon." *Southwestern Journal of Theology* 27,
no. 2 (Spring 1985): 32–37.

Frick, Murray. *Reach the Back Row: Creative Approaches for
High-Impact Preaching*. Loveland, CO: Group Publishing
Vital Ministry, 1999.

Greidanus, Sidney. *The Modern Preacher and the Ancient Text*.
Grand Rapids: Eerdmans, 1988.

Henderson, David. "Bringing the Truth to Bear on Our World."
Preaching 14, no. 4 (March–April 1999): 26–32.

Hogan, Lucy Lind, and Robert Reid. *Connecting with the Congregation: Rhetoric and the Art of Preaching*. Nashville:
Abingdon Press, 1999.

Holmes, Zan. "Enabling the Word to Happen." In *Power in the Pulpit: How America's Most Effective Black Preachers Prepare Their Sermons*, edited by Cloephus J. LaRue, 74–88. Louisville: Westminster John Knox Press, 2002.

Howe, Reuel L. *Partners in Preaching: Clergy and Laity in Dialogue*. New York: Seabury Press, 1967.

Hybels, Bill. "The Accompanying Presence." *Leadership* 25, no. 2 (Spring 2004): 45–47.

Jackson, Edgar N. *How to Preach to People's Needs*. Grand Rapids: Baker, 1976.

Jackson, Richard. "Preaching to Change Lives." In *Communicate with Power*, edited by Michael Duduit, 83–89. Grand Rapids: Baker, 1996.

Jeter, Joseph R., and Ronald J. Allen. *One Gospel, Many Ears: Preaching for Different Listeners in the Congregation*. St. Louis: Chalice Press, 2002.

Johnston, Graham. *Preaching to a Postmodern World*. Grand Rapids: Baker, 2001.

Jones, Brian. "Application in Biblical Preaching." Doctor of Ministry Thesis Project, Gordon-Conwell Theological Seminary, 2003.

Kaiser, Walter C., and Moises Silva. *An Introduction to Biblical Hermeneutics: The Search for Meaning*. Grand Rapids: Zondervan, 1994.

Killinger, John. *Fundamentals of Preaching*. Philadelphia: Fortress Press, 1985.

———. *Preaching the New Millennium*. Nashville: Abingdon Press, 1999.

Kuhatschek, Jack. *Taking the Guesswork Out of Applying the Bible*. Downer's Grove, IL: InterVarsity Press, 1990.

LaRue, Cloephus J., ed. *Power in the Pulpit: How America's Most Effective Black Preachers Prepare Their Sermons*. Louisville: Westminster John Knox Press, 2002.

Lewis, Ralph L., and Gregg Lewis. *Inductive Preaching: Helping People Listen*. Wheaton, IL: Crossway Books, 1983.

Litfin, Duane. "Felt-Needs Preaching." *PreachingToday.com*. http://www.preachingtoday.com/skills/audioworkshops/ pt245b.html (accessed June 27, 2008).

Long, Thomas G. *Preaching and the Literary Forms of the Bible*. Philadelphia: Fortress Press, 1989.

———. *The Witness of Preaching*. Louisville: Westminster John Knox Press, 1989.

Loscalzo, Craig A. *Evangelistic Preaching That Connects: Guidance in Shaping Fresh and Appealing Sermons*. Downer's Grove, IL: Intervarsity Press, 1995.

———. *Preaching Sermons That Connect: Effective Communication Through Identification*. Downer's Grove, IL: Intervarsity Press, 1992.

Lose, David J. *Confessing Jesus Christ: Preaching in a Postmodern World*. Grand Rapids: Eerdmans, 2003.

Mains, David. "From Applications to Action." *Leadership* 7, no. 4 (Fall 1986): 64–68.

———. "Killer Applications." *Leadership* 5, no. 2 (Spring 2004): 43–44.

Malphurs, Aubrey. *Doing Church: A Biblical Guide for Leading Ministries Through Change*. Grand Rapids: Kregel, 1999.

Massey, James Earl. "Application in the Sermon." In *Handbook of Contemporary Preaching*, edited by Michael Duduit, 209–14. Nashville: Broadman Press, 1992.

McClure, John S. *The Round-Table Pulpit: Where Leadership and Preaching Meet*. Nashville: Abingdon Press, 1995.

McDill, Wayne. *The 12 Essential Skills for Great Preaching*. Nashville: Broadman and Holman, 1994.

Miller, Calvin. *The Empowered Communicator: Keys to Unlocking an Audience*. Nashville: Broadman and Holman, 1994.

———. *Marketplace Preaching: How to Return the Sermon to Where It Belongs*. Grand Rapids: Baker, 1995.

———. *Preaching: The Art of Narrative Exposition*. Grand Rapids: Baker, 2006.

Olford, Stephen F., and David L. Olford. *Anointed Expository Preaching*. Nashville: Broadman and Holman, 1998.

Ortberg, John. "Biblical Preaching Is About Life Change, Not Sermon Form." *PreachingToday.com*. http://www.preaching today.com/skills/style/200008.13.html (accessed June 26, 2008).

Pentz, Victor D. "Preaching to Effect Transformation." Doctor of Ministry Dissertation, Fuller Theological Seminary, 1991.

Quicke, Michael. "Applying God's Word in a Secular Culture." *Preaching* no. 4 (January–February 2002): 7–15.

Read, David H. C. *Preaching About the Needs of Real People*. Philadelphia: Westminster Press, 1988.

Richard, Ramesh P. "Application Theory in Relation to the New Testament." *Bibliotheca Sacra* 143, no. 571 (April–June 1986): 205–17.

Robinson, Haddon. *Biblical Preaching: The Development and Delivery of Expository Messages*, 2nd ed. Grand Rapids: Baker, 2001.

———. *Biblical Sermons: How Twelve Preachers Apply the Principles of Biblical Preaching*. Grand Rapids: Baker, 1989.

———. "Blending Bible Content and Life Application." *PreachingToday.com*, January, 2000. http://www.preachingtoday.com/index.taf?_UserReference+7A9C2DE641A3FB63F9EC327&_function=journal&_op=article&res=200001.2 (accessed October 8, 2003).

———. "Grace and Truth in Application." *PreachingToday.com*, December 1999. http://www.preachingtoday.com/index.taf?_UserReference=7A9C2DE641A3F9B63F9EC327&_function=journal&_op=article&res=199903.2 (accessed October 28, 2003).

———. "The Heresy of Application." In *The Art and Craft of Biblical Preaching: A Comprehensive Resource for Today's Communicators*, edited by Haddon Robinson and Craig Brian Larson, 306–11. Grand Rapids: Zondervan, 2005.

————. "The Heresy of Application." *Leadership* 18, no. 4 (Fall 1997): 21–27.

————. "No Application Necessary." *PreachingToday.com.* June, 2000. http://www.preachingtoday.com/index.taf?_User Reference==7A9C2DE641A3F9B63F9EC327&_function= journal&_op=article&res=200006.2 (accessed October 28, 2003).

————. "The Preacher and the Message." Class notes, Gordon-Conwell Theological Seminary, May 2002.

————. "What Authority Does a Preacher Have Anymore?" In *Mastering Contemporary Preaching*, edited by Marshall Shelley, 17–26. Portland, OR: Multnomah and Christianity Today, 1989.

Russell, Robert. "Application: The Key to Relevant Preaching." Audiotape of workshop presented at the National Preaching Summit, Indianapolis, 2000. Bridgeport, IL: Christian Audio Tapes, 2000.

Self, William L. "Preaching to Joe Secular." In *Communicate with Power*, edited by Michael Duduit, 170–76. Grand Rapids: Baker, 1996.

Stott, John. *Between Two Worlds: The Art of Preaching in the Twentieth Century*. Grand Rapids: Eerdmans, 1982.

Sunukjian, Donald R. *Invitation to Biblical Preaching: Proclaiming Truth With Clarity and Relevance*. Grand Rapids: Kregel, 2007.

————. "Questions That Put Muscles on Bones (Part 5)." *PreachingToday.com*, September 2003. http://www.preachingtoday .com/index.taf?_userreference=7A9C2DE641A3F9B63F 9EC327&_function=journal&_op=article&res=200303.20 (accessed October 28, 2003).

Veerman, David. "Apply Within." In *The Art and Craft of Biblical Preaching: A Comprehensive Resource for Today's Communicators*, edited by Haddon Robinson and Craig Brian Larson. Grand Rapids: Zondervan, 2005: 283–88.

————. "Making Applications Personal." In *Changing Lives*

Through Preaching and Worship, edited by Marshall Shelley. Nashville: Moorings of Random House, 1995: 59–70.

Warren, Rick. "Preaching for Life Change: It's All in Learning to Preach Like Jesus." *Preaching* 19, no. 2 (September–October 2003): 9–19.

———. "Purpose-Driven Preaching: An Interview with Rick Warren." By Michael Duduit. *Preaching* 17, no. 2 (September–October 2001): 6–32.

Wenig, Scott. "Life-Changing Application." *PreachingToday.com*, April 2000. http://www.preachingtoday.com/Index.Taf?_User reference=7a9c2de641a3f9b63f9ec327&_Function= Journal&_Op=Article&Res=200004.3 (accessed October 28, 2003).

Whitney, Donald. "The Development of the Use of Application in the Preaching at Glenfield Baptist Church." Doctor of Ministry Thesis Project, Trinity Evangelical Divinity School, 1987.

Wiersbe, Warren. *The Dynamics of Preaching*. Grand Rapids: Baker, 1999.

Wilhite, Keith. "A Sneak Peek at the Point: Sermon Introductions That Aim at Application." *Preaching* 5, no. 6 (May–June 1990): 17–22.

Willimon, William H. *The Intrusive Word: Preaching to the Unbaptized*. Grand Rapids: Eerdmans, 1994.

———. *Pastor: A Reader for Ordained Ministry*. Nashville: Abingdon Press, 2002.

———. *Peculiar Speech: Preaching to the Baptized*. Grand Rapids: Eerdmans, 1992.

Wimberly, John W. "Preaching to a Changing, Changed Church." *Living Pulpit* 9, no. 4 (October–December 2000): 40–41.

York, Hershael W., and Scott A. Blue. "Is Application Necessary in the Expository Sermon?" *Southern Baptist Journal of Theology* 3, no. 2 (Summer 1999): 70–84.

PREACHING RESOURCES FROM
KREGEL ACADEMIC & PROFESSIONAL

Creating Stories That Connect
A Pastor's Guide to Storytelling
D. Bruce Seymour

This innovative book helps pastors and teachers enhance their teaching with original, audience-appropriate stories—the way Jesus did! Seymour explains how such stories work, when to use them, and how to create them.
978-0-8254-3671-0 • Paperback • 144 pages

Planning Your Preaching
A Step-by-Step Guide for Developing a One-Year Preaching Calendar
Stephen Nelson Rummage

This practical guide provides a systematic and proven method for planning a cohesive preaching ministry a year in advance.
978-0-8254-3648-2 • Paperback • 240 pages

Using Old Testament Hebrew in Preaching
A Guide for Students and Pastors
Paul D. Wegner

Wegner emphasizes the importance of using Hebrew in preparation for preaching and offers a detailed process for moving from text to exegesis to proclamation.
978-0-8254-3936-0 • Paperback • 176 pages

Invitation to Theological Studies Series
Invitation to Biblical Preaching
Proclaiming Truth with Clarity and Relevance
Donald R. Sunukjian

Invitation to Biblical Preaching takes the reader step-by-step through the entire process of preparing a biblical message, from studying a passage with skill and integrity to delivering a message with persuasion, accuracy, passion, and relevance.
978-0-8254-3666-6 • Hardcover • 376 pages

PREACHING WITH SERIES FROM
KREGEL ACADEMIC & PROFESSIONAL

Preaching with Conviction
Connecting with Postmodern Listeners
Kenton C. Anderson;
foreword by Michael Duduit

978-0-8254-2020-7 • Paperback • 160 pages

Preaching with Freshness
Bruce Mawhinney;
foreword by Jay E. Adams

978-0-8254-3449-5 • Paperback • 264 pages

Preaching with Integrity
Kenton C. Anderson;
foreword by Craig Larson

978-0-8254-2021-4 • Paperback • 144 pages

Preaching with Passion
Alex Montoya;
foreword by John MacArthur

978-0-8254-3366-5 • Paperback • 160 pages

Preaching with Relevance
Without Dumbing Down
Keith Willhite;
foreword by Haddon Robinson

978-0-8254-4114-1 • Paperback • 144 pages

Preaching with Variety
How to Re-create the Dynamics of Biblical Genres
Jeffery Arthurs;
foreword by Haddon Robinson

978-0-8254-2019-1 • Paperback • 240 pages